TABLE OF CONTENTS

INTRODUCTION

Welcome to "Essential Diabetic Cookbook for Beginners 2025 Edition", where health and taste coexist harmoniously in every recipe. This cookbook is designed for those navigating the complexities of diabetes, but it's more than just a collection of recipes. It's a celebration of flavors, textures, and colors that cater to your health needs without sacrificing enjoyment.

Living with diabetes often means adhering to strict dietary guidelines, which can sometimes lead to the misconception that diabetic-friendly meals are bland or restrictive. Our mission is to dispel this myth. This book is a testament to the creativity and diversity that can thrive within the boundaries of a diabetic diet. Each recipe has been crafted with careful consideration of glycemic index, carbohydrate content, and nutritional balance, ensuring they are both safe and satisfying for those with diabetes.

We've curated a diverse range of recipes that cater to various tastes and dietary preferences, from comforting classics to innovative creations. Whether you're craving a hearty breakfast, a light lunch, a nourishing dinner, or even a delectable dessert, you'll find options here that align with your dietary needs and delight your palate.

Moreover, this book is more than just a cookbook. It's a resource that educates and empowers. Alongside the recipes, you'll find tips on managing blood sugar levels, understanding food labels, and making smart food choices.

Types of Diabetes

Diabetes comes in a variety of forms, each with special traits and needs for care. When putting together a diabetic recipe book, it is vital to comprehend these kinds. Here's a quick rundown:

Diabetes Type 1

An autoimmune disease in which there is little to no insulin production by the pancreas. While it is typically detected in children and teenagers, it can appear at any age. Insulin treatment is typically required for management.

Type 2 Diabetes

The most prevalent type is when the body finally loses its capacity to make adequate insulin due to improper insulin utilization, or insulin resistance.

They are frequently linked to physical inactivity, obesity, and family history. Changes in lifestyle, oral medicines, and occasionally insulin are all part of management.

Gestational Diabetes

Pregnancy causes the development of gestational diabetes, which often goes away after delivery. increases the likelihood of problems for the mother and the child as well as the long-term risk of type 2 diabetes they are controlled with food, exercise, and occasionally medicine.

Prediabetes

Despite being higher than normal, the blood sugar levels do not meet the criteria for type 2 diabetes.

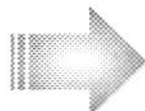

Other Specific Types

Including monogenic diabetes, cystic fibrosis-related diabetes, and others caused by specific conditions or syndromes.

Effectiveness of a Diabetic Recipe Book

A diabetic recipe book can be highly effective in managing diabetes for several reasons:

Nutritional Balance

Provides recipes with a balanced mix of macronutrients (carbohydrates, proteins, fats) and micronutrients, crucial for blood sugar control. *Carbohydrate Management:* Offers recipes with a focus on low glycemic index foods and controlled carbohydrate portions, aiding in blood glucose stabilization.

Healthy Eating Habits

Encourages overall healthy eating patterns, which are vital for managing body weight and improving insulin sensitivity.

Dietary Variety

Introduces a variety of foods and flavors, making the dietary restrictions of diabetes more manageable and enjoyable, which can improve adherence to a healthy diet.

Educational Tool

Provides nutritional education, helping readers understand how different foods affect blood sugar levels and offer guidance on portion control and meal planning.

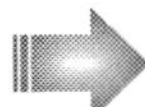

Customization for Individual Needs

Can offer options for personalizing recipes to fit individual nutritional needs and preferences, acknowledging that diabetes management is not one-size-fits-all.

Supports Overall Health

By focusing on whole, unprocessed foods, these recipes can also support cardiovascular health, weight management, and overall well-being.

WHAT FOODS IN A DIABETIC DIET?

Allowed Foods

When managing diabetes, it's crucial to focus on foods that help maintain stable blood sugar levels while providing essential nutrients. Below is a list of foods considered suitable for a diabetic diet:

 **Whole Grains**

Examples: Brown rice, whole wheat, quinoa, oats, barley, and whole grain bread and pasta are all examples of healthy grains.

Benefits: Higher in fiber and have a lower glycemic index compared to refined grains.

 **Vegetables**

Non-starchy: veggies including broccoli, cauliflower, carrots, peppers, and leafy greens (spinach, kale).

Starchy: In moderation, like sweet potatoes, corn, and peas. Benefits: Rich in vitamins, minerals, and fiber, and low in calories.

 **Fruits**

Examples: Berries, apples, pears, oranges, and peaches.

Note: While fruits contain natural sugars, they also provide essential nutrients and fiber. Portion control is key.

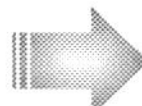 **Proteins**

Lean Meat: Lean meats like chicken, turkey, and lean cuts of beef and pork, as well Fish: as fish—particularly fatty fish high in omega-3 fatty acids like sardines, mackerel, and salmon—are recommended.

Plant-Based Proteins: Beans, lentils, chickpeas, tofu, and tempeh.

Benefits: Essential for muscle health and satiety without impacting blood sugar levels significantly.

 **Dairy Alternatives**

Low-Fat Dairy: Milk, cheese, and yogurt.

Non-Dairy Alternatives: Unsweetened almond milk, soy milk, and coconut milk. Benefits: Source of calcium and protein. Choose low-fat options and be mindful of added sugars in flavored products.

 **Healthy Fats**

Sources: Include avocados, nuts, seeds, olive oil, and other plant-based oils in your diet.

Benefits: These sources are essential for heart health and can contribute to a feeling of fullness. However, they are calorie-dense, so moderation is essential.

 **Legumes**

Examples: Beans, lentils, chickpeas.

Benefits: Good source of plant-based protein and fiber, helping with blood sugar control.

 **Herbs and Spices**

Examples: Garlic, cinnamon, turmeric, and other fresh or dried herbs. Benefits: Adds flavor without adding sugar or salt.

General tips on eating permitted foods

Patients with diabetes should follow a balanced diet that limits their daily calorie intake to 45–60% carbs, preferably those that are high in fibres and have a low glycemic index. They should also restrict their intake of simple sugars to 5–10%, lipids to 20–35 %, and protein to 10–25%.

High sugar content and concentrated carbohydrates can lead to blood sugar spikes. Managing a diabetic diet involves balancing permitted foods that support blood sugar control with the cautious intake of foods that can negatively impact glucose levels. Hereare some general guidelines:

- **Prioritize Low Glycemic Index Foods**: Choose foods that have a minimal impact on blood sugar levels, such as whole grains, legumes, and most vegetables.
- **Incorporate Fiber-Rich Foods:** High-fiber foods, like vegetables, nuts, seeds, and whole grains, can help slow down glucose absorption and improve blood sugar control. *Choose Healthy Fats:* Incorporate unsaturated fat sources, which help strengthen heart health without raising blood sugar levels: avocados, nuts, seeds, and olive oil.
- Lean Proteins are Key: Opt for lean protein sources like chicken, fish, tofu, and legumes, as they have minimal impact on blood sugar.
- **Control Portion Sizes:** Even with healthier choices, it's important to watch portion sizes to manage blood sugar and weight.
- **Stay Hydrated:** Limit sugar-filled beverages and drink lots of water as these might lead to sharp rises in blood sugar levels.
- **Regular Meal Times:** Limit sugar-filled beverages and drink lots of water as these might lead to sharp rises in blood sugar levels.

Forbidden Foods

No foods are really forbidden, but some people may want to limit their use because of their possible impact on sugar levels. Here is a list of them:

 **High Glycemic Index Foods**

Examples: White bread, white rice, and other refined grains; sugary cereals. Reason: These foods can cause rapid spikes in blood sugar levels.

 **Sugary Foods and Beverages**

Examples: Soda, candy, desserts, pastries, and sweetened beverages.

Reason: High in sugar and often in empty calories, contributing to blood sugar spikes.

 **Processed Snacks**

Examples: Chips, cookies, and snack cakes.

Reason: Often high in refined carbs, sugars, and unhealthy fats.

 **Trans Fats**

Sources: Margarine, shortening, and some processed foods. Reason:

Unhealthy for heart health, which is a concern for diabetics.

-Fat Dairy Products

Examples: Whole milk, full-fat cheese, and ice cream.

Reason: High in saturated fats, which can affect cardiovascular health.

Fatty Meats

Examples: Bacon, ribs, and other high-fat cuts of meat.

Reason: High in saturated fats, contributing to heart disease risk.

Fried Foods

Examples: Fried chicken, French fries, and doughnuts.

Reason: Typically high in calories, unhealthy fats, and can contribute to weight gain.

Alcohol

Note: Moderate consumption might be okay for some, but it's important to check with a healthcare provider.

Reason: Can cause blood sugar fluctuations and interact with diabetes medications.

High-Sodium Foods

Examples: Canned soups, pickles, and processed meats.

Reason: Excessive sodium can exacerbate hypertension, common in diabetics.

Certain Fruit Juices and Dried Fruits

Reason: High sugar content and concentrated carbohydrates can lead to blood sugar spikes.

General tips on eating prohibited foods

- **Limit Sugary Foods and Beverages:** Reduce intake of foods high in added sugars, like sweets, desserts, and sugary drinks.
- **Avoid Trans and Saturated Fats:** Avoid consuming foods rich in unhealthy fats, such as deep-fried items, full-fat dairy products, and fatty meats.
- **Reduce Refined Carbohydrates:** Cut down on white bread, pastries, and other refined grains that can cause rapid blood sugar spikes.
- **Moderate Alcohol Consumption:** If alcohol is consumed, it should be in moderation and preferably with food to avoid hypoglycemia.
- **Be Cautious with Salt:** Excessive salt intake can be harmful, especially for those with diabetes-related hypertension.
- **Balance and Moderation:** If consuming higher-risk foods, balance them with healthier options and keep the portions small.
- **Read Food Labels:** Understanding food labels can help identify hidden sugars, unhealthy fats, and excessive carbohydrates.
- **Consult Health Professionals:** Individuals with diabetes must consult with healthcare providers or dietitians for personalized dietary advice.

READ THE LABELS

Important details about the nutritional makeup of packaged meals and beverages can be found on food labels. Reading food labels is crucial for anyone on a diabetic diet for several reasons:

Carbohydrate content: Controlling the amount of carbohydrates consumed is essential for managing diabetes since they have a major impact on blood sugar levels. The total amount of carbohydrates in each serving, including sugars and dietary fiber, is listed on food labels. People with diabetes can better control their blood sugar levels by checking their carbohydrate intake with the use of this information.

Sugars: Food labels make a distinction between added sugars and natural sugars, which are present in components like fruit (sugars added during food processing). Limiting added sugar consumption is recommended for diabetics since too much sugar can cause blood glucose levels to increase.

Artificial sweeteners, sometimes referred to as artificial sugars or sugar substitutes, are man-made substances that are added to food and drink to replace sugar. These sweeteners are often used by people, including those with diabetes, to cut back on calories or sugar intake, or as an alternative to natural sugar in meals.

Here are a few popular sugar substitutes:

- **Aspartame (commercial brands: NutraSweet, Equal):** *One* of the most popular artificial sweeteners, aspartame is frequently found in sugar-free confectionery, chewing gum, and beverages. It is not appropriate for cooking at high temperatures because it is heat-sensitive.
- **One of the first artificial sweeteners, saccharin (brand names):** Sweet'N Low, Sweet Twin, Necta Sweet) is frequently included in diet sodas and tabletop sweeteners. It is calorie-free.
- **Sucralose, often known as Splenda:** Sucralose can be used in baking and cooking because it is heat stable. It is frequently present in a large variety of reduced- and sugar-free products.
- **Stevia (brand names:** Truvia, Stevia in the Raw, Pure Via): Stevia is a naturally occurring sweetener derived from the leaves of the stevia plant. It is used in many different dishes and beverages and is many times sweeter than sugar.
- **Acesulfame potassium:** Sometimes known as Ace-K or Acesulfame K, is a common artificial sweetener that is used with other sweeteners to boost sweetness. It is often used in sugar-free beverages and desserts and is heat-stable. Neotame, sometimes known as New tame, is a more recent artificial sweetener that is used in a range of culinary goods. Though heat-stable, it shares chemical similarities with aspartame.
- **Cyclamate:** Cyclamate is used in several foreign countries, while not being allowed for usage in the United States. It often performs admirably in concoctions with other sweeteners.
- **Advantame:** Used in many culinary goods, Advantame is a relatively new artificial sweetener. It has a lot more sweetness than aspartame.

Artificial sweeteners in the US must pass rigorous safety testing conducted by the Food and Drug Administration before being approved for use in foods and beverages (FDA).

Each person may have a different tolerance for various artificial sweeteners, and some may find some to be more flavorful than others. When deciding whether to use artificial sweeteners, it's important to consult a trained a healthcare provider because some people may have negative side effects or be concerned about long-term health effects.

- **Fiber:** Dietary fiber lowers blood sugar levels by slowing down the absorption of carbohydrates. Dietary fiber content is shown on food labels, allowing consumers to choose meals that are high in fiber and low in net carbs.
- **Serving Size:** A key part of part management is being aware of your serving size. Recommendation serving sizes are listed on food labels, which helps consumers control part sizes and prevent overindulging.
- **Calories:** Keeping track of calories consumed is crucial for managing weight, which in turn affects the control of diabetes. Calorie counts on food labels assist consumers in making decisions about how much energy they consume from meals and snacks.
- **Fat Content:** Saturated, trans, and unsaturated fats are among the different forms of fat listed on food labels. Limiting saturated and trans fats is advised for those with diabetes since they may worsen heart health issues.
- ***Sodium:*** Consuming excessive amounts of sodium can raise blood pressure, which many diabetics find concerning. People can select low-sodium options by reading food labels, which list the sodium content per serving.
- **Ingredient List:** All of the ingredients of a product are listed on food labels, typically in decreasing order of quantity. This aids in the identification of allergies, bad fats, and hidden sugars that might be interfering with the control of diabetes.
- **Allergies:** Common allergens, including dairy, gluten, nuts, and soy, are also included on food labels. It's critical to take care of your allergies in addition to your diabetes for general wellness.
- **Glycemic Index (GI):** Although it's not often included on food labels, some goods might have this data. People with diabetes can make decisions that affect their blood sugar levels more gradually by having a better understanding of GI.

FOOD NUTRITIONAL TABLES

Nutritional information serves a crucial role in promoting public health and empowering consumers to make informed dietary choices. One of the most significant reasons for its importance is its role in addressing the growing concerns about diet-related health issues, including obesity, diabetes, heart disease, and other chronic illnesses.

Firstly, this information provides transparency and accountability in the food industry. They offer consumers a clear understanding of what they are purchasing, enabling them to assess the nutritional value of the product and make conscious decisions. This transparency encourages food manufacturers to produce healthier options as they are aware that consumers are increasingly scrutinizing the nutritional content of their products.

Moreover, nutritional information supports individuals in managing their dietary intake, particularly in calorie control. The serving size and calorie information allow consumers to gauge how the product fits into their daily caloric needs. This knowledge is vital for those striving to maintain a balanced diet and manage their weight effectively.

Additionally, promotes dietary diversity and balanced nutrition. By displaying the amounts of various nutrients like fats, carbohydrates, protein, and vitamins, they encourage individuals to diversify their diets and ensure they are obtaining a wide range of nutrients. People can tailor their choices to meet specific dietary requirements, whether they are focusing on low-fat options, increasing fiber intake, or reducing sugar consumption.

Furthermore, nutritional tables are valuable tools for individuals with specific dietary restrictions or health conditions. Those with allergies or intolerances can quickly identify potential allergens in a product, reducing the risk of adverse reactions. People with conditions like diabetes can monitor their carbohydrate intake, while those with heart conditions can assess sodium and saturated fat levels.

Nutrition tables or nutrition labels on food packaging provide a summary of essential nutritional values for a specific food product. These values typically include:

Serving Size: The recommended portion size for the food item, which help consumers understand how the nutritional values apply to the amount they are likely to consume.

- **Calories:** The total energy content of one serving of the food product, measured in calories or kilocalories (kcal).
- **Total Fat:** The total amount of fat in one serving, often broken down into subcategories like saturated and trans fats.
- **Cholesterol:** The amount of cholesterol in one serving.
- **Sodium:** The quantity of sodium (salt) in one serving.
- **Total Carbohydrate:** The total amount of carbohydrates in one serving, further divided into dietary fiber and sugars.
- **Protein:** The amount of protein in one serving.
- **Vitamins and Minerals:** The percentages of daily recommended values for vitamins and minerals, such as vitamin D, calcium, iron, and potassium, may be found on some labels.
- **Percent Daily Values (DV):** Based on a 2,000 or 2,500-calorie diet, these percentages show how much one serving of the product adds to a daily diet. It aids customers in comprehending the importance of the nutrients in their regular use.
- **Additional Information:** Nutrition labels may also include specific details about allergens, ingredients, and manufacturer contact information.

In essence, food nutritional tables promote public health by providing valuable information to consumers, enabling them to make healthier choices, and incentivizing the food industry to produce more nutritious products. This information plays a pivotal role in addressing the global health challenges associated with diet-related diseases and empowering individuals to take control of their nutrition. As such, they are a fundamental component of a modern food system that prioritizes health and well-being. For more information and details on the nutritional values of foods, consult the Wikipedia page "Table of food nutrients"

SHOPPING LIST

A shopping list is a valuable tool for a person on a diabetic diet for several important reasons:

- **Meal Planning:** A shopping list helps individuals plan their meals. Listing the ingredients needed for specific diabetic-friendly recipes ensures that they have everything required to prepare balanced and nutritious meals.
- **Portion Control:** A shopping list can include portion sizes, which is essential for managing blood sugar levels. By purchasing the right quantities of ingredients, individuals can avoid overeating and maintain portion control.
- **Nutritional Balance:** Diabetes management involves monitoring carbohydrate intake, fiber, fats, and other nutrients. A shopping list can be organized to ensure a balance of these nutrients, making it easier to meet dietary goals.
- **Avoiding Impulse** *Purchases:* With a well-structured shopping list, individuals are less likely to make impulse purchases of unhealthy snacks or high-sugar foods that can negatively impact blood sugar levels.
- **Efficiency:** A shopping list streamlines the grocery shopping process. It saves time by guiding shoppers through the store to find the items they need and prevents them from wandering the aisles aimlessly.
- **Budgeting:** Creating a shopping list can help individuals stick to their budget. By planning meals and only purchasing the items on the list, they can avoid overspending on unnecessary items.
- **Variety:** For the sake of general health and meal satisfaction, a shopping list can guarantee variety in the diabetic diet by incorporating a wide selection of fruits, vegetables, lean proteins, and nutritious grains.
- **Food Safety:** When planning meals and creating a shopping list, individuals can also consider food safety by ensuring they have fresh ingredients and avoiding items that may have expired.

In summary, a shopping list is a practical tool that supports individuals with diabetes in making informed and health-conscious food choices, managing portion sizes, and staying organized while grocery shopping. It plays a vital role in helping individuals adhere to their diabetic diet plan and maintain stable blood sugar levels.

Shopping list according to recipes

- Proteins:
  - Eggs
  - Chicken (boneless, skinless)
  - Salmon fillets
  - White fish (e.g. cod or tilapia)
  - Free-range turkey
  - Shrimp
  - Tofu
- Cereals and grains:
  - Quinoa
  - Lentils
  - Oats
  - brown rice
  - Barley
- Vegetables:
  - Spinach
  - Mushrooms
  - Asparagus

- Cauliflower
- Broccoli
- Zucchinis
- Peppers
- Eggplant
- Green beans
- Tomatoes
- Cabbage
- Cucumber
- Butternut squash

➔ Fruit:

- Berries (e.g. strawberries, blueberries, raspberries)
- Avocado
- Lemons
- Apples
- Pears
- kalamata olives

➔ Dairy alternatives:

- Greek yogurt
- Almond milk
- Feta cheese
- Milk from coconuts (for chia pudding)

➔ Nuts and seeds:

- almonds
- Nuts
- Chia seeds

➔ Basic pantry items:

- Olive oil
- Balsamic vinegar
- Garlic
- Onions
- Herbs and spices (e.g. cinnamon, dill, basil, turmeric, ginger)
- Low sodium chicken or vegetable broth
- Tomato sauce
- Peanut butter (or almond butter)
- Sugar-free sweetener (if needed)
- Flax Seeds (if not already in the bread)

➔ Baking ingredients (for bread and muffins):

- Almond flour
- Coconut flour
- Flax Seed meal
- Wholemeal flour
- Baking powder
- Sodium bicarbonate

➔ Drinks:

- Green tea
- Ginger
- Turmeric
- Tea bags (for cold herbal teas)
- sparkling water

➔ Other:

- Protein powder (if desired for shakes)
- Almond butter (for almond butter balls)

JUST STARTING OUT? NO WORRIES

If you are handy in the kitchen, you could skip this chapter, although a refresher never hurts.

While For a kitchen beginner, several essential tools can make the learning process easier and cooking more enjoyable and safe. Here's a basic list:

- **Good Quality Knife Set**: A chef's, bread, and utility knife are crucial. Could you make sure they are well-sharpened?
- **Cutting Board**: Preferably in wood or plastic to protect your knife blades and provide a stable surface for chopping.
- **Pans and Pots**: At least one non-stick frying pan and a medium-sized pot are essential. Choose pots with a good base for even heat distribution.
- **Ladles, Spatulas, and Spoons**: Various utensils for stirring, flipping, and serving. Materials like silicone or wood are ideal as they don't scratch the surfaces of pots and pans.
- **Mixing Bowls and Measuring Cups**: Useful for preparing ingredients before starting to cook and for mixing dough or salads.
- **Kitchen Scale and Measuring Spoons**: Accurately measuring ingredients is especially important in baking.
- **Peeler and Grater**: For easily peeling fruits and vegetables and grating cheeses or vegetables.
- **Kitchen Timer**: It helps keep track of cooking times, especially for beginners who are still learning how to calculate cooking times.
- **Kitchen Thermometer**: This is important to control the cooking of meat and ensure food safety.
- **Bottle Opener and Can Opener**: Essential for opening various types of packaging.

You can prepare a wide range of dishes and develop your cooking skills by starting with these basic tools. You can add specialized tools to your arsenal as you gain experience.

Also, starting with simpler cooking methods and dishes is a great way to build confidence and skill. Here are some cooking options along with the essential tools you may need:

 **Boil and simmer**

Dishes: Pasta, rice, boiled eggs, simple soups.

Tools: pot, slotted spoon, colander.

 **Saute and fry**

Dishes: sauteed vegetables, stir-fried dishes, plain meat, or tofu stir-fries.

Tools: non-stick pan or wok, spatula, tongs.

 **Cooking**

Dishes: Simple cakes, biscuits, roasted vegetables, baked chicken or fish.

Tools: baking tray, baking tray, bowls, measuring cups and spoons, oven gloves.

 **Grill and roast**

Dishes: Grilled chicken, hamburgers, grilled vegetables.

Tools: grill or baking pan, tongs, basting brush.

Steam cooking

Dishes: Steamed vegetables, steamed fish, dumplings.

Utensils: steamer basket or pot, water pot.

 **Slow cooking**

Dishes: Stews, slow-cooked meats, soups.

Tools: Slow Cooker.

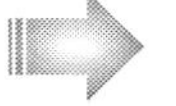 **Frying in a pan**

Dishes: pancakes, fried eggs, simple meat or fish fillets.

Tools: non-stick pan, spatula, cooking oil, or butter.

Tips for Beginners

- **Start simple:** Start with recipes that have fewer ingredients and steps.
- **Read the recipe carefully:** Understand the steps before you start.
- **Preparation before cooking:** Measure and chop the ingredients in advance.
- **Temperature Control:** Learn to adjust stove heat for different cooking methods.
- **Taste as you go:** Develop your palate by tasting and adjusting seasonings.

By starting with these types of cooking, the beginner will be able to gradually learn different techniques and gain confidence in cooking. The key is to create simple, practice regularly, and avoid making mistakes, as they are part of the learning pro.

Recipe structure

The recipes in this guide consist of a list of ingredients with relative quantities, from the step-by-step preparation instructions to the nutritional values, which are necessarily approximate because they can vary depending on the weight of the ingredients used (e.g. a 50 g egg has different values than an 80 g egg); by times and servings.
It is important to note that the (approximate) nutritional values of recipes are calculated by analyzing the specific nutritional values of each food for their quantities. The product of this value is multiplied by the recipe's number of servings. Finally, remember that the nutritional value of ingredients may vary depending on brand, freshness and how prepared.

Scrambled Eggs

Time: *5 min* ***Cook:*** *10 min* ***Servings****: 2*

Ingredients:

- Large eggs: 4 (preferably organic or pasture-raised)
- Unsweetened almond milk: 2 tbsp (or skim milk)
- Olive oil: 1 tsp (or a small amount of cooking spray)
- Baby spinach: 1 cup, chopped
- Cherry tomatoes: 6-8, halved
- Red onion: ¼ small, finely chopped (optional)
- Fresh herbs: 1 tbsp, chopped (such as parsley or chives)
- Low-sodium salt: 1 pinch (optional, based on your sodium needs)
- Black pepper: to taste
- Avocado: ½ avocado, sliced optional garnish for healthy fats)

Instructions:

1. Crack the eggs into a small bowl, add the almond milk and whisk until the eggs are well combined and slightly frothy. This will give your eggs a light, fluffy texture.
2. Heat 1 teaspoon of olive oil in a non-stick frying pan over medium heat. Add the red onion (if using) and saute for 2-3 minutes until softened.
3. Add the baby spinach and cherry tomatoes, cooking for 1-2 minutes until the spinach is slightly wilted and the tomatoes are softened. Remove the vegetables from the pan and set aside.
4. In the same pan, reduce the heat to low and pour in the beaten eggs, stirring gently and continuously with a spatula. This will ensure soft, creamy scrambled eggs. After about 2-3 minutes, when the eggs are almost cooked (slightly runny), add the sauteed vegetables and herbs, and cook for another 1-2 minutes until the eggs are completely set but still soft.
5. Remove from heat and plate the scrambled eggs, garnishing with avocado slices.
6. Season with salt (optional) and black pepper to taste.

Variants and substitutions:

Include high-fiber vegetables like mushrooms, zucchini, or bell peppers to increase satiety and help regulate blood sugar. Add a pinch of cayenne pepper or red pepper flakes for a little kick, which can also help boost your metabolism.

Nutritional information (per serving): Calories: 240 kcal; Protein: 15g; Fat: 18g; Net Carbs: 7g; Sugar: 3g; Cholesterol 325mg; Sodium 200mg; Potassium: 480mg.

High-Fiber Whole Grain Cereal

Time: *5 min* ***Cook:*** *20 min* ***Servings****: 2*

Ingredients:

- Rolled oats: ½ cup
- Water: 1 ½ cups (or unsweetened almond milk)
- Ground flax Seeds: 1 tbsp
- Chia seeds: 1 tbsp (optional)
- Mixed nuts: 2 tbsp, chopped (such as almonds, walnuts, or pecans)
- Fresh or frozen berries: ½ cup (such as blueberries, raspberries, or strawberries)
- Unsweetened coconut flakes: 1 tablespoon (optional for flavor)
- Cinnamon: ½ teaspoon (adds flavor without sugar)
- Vanilla extract: ½ tsp (optional for added flavor)
- Low-sodium salt: a pinch (optional)
- Sweetener (optional): Use a low-glycemic sweetener such as stevia, monk fruit, or a small amount of honey/maple syrup.

Instructions:

1. In a medium saucepan, bring 1 ½ cups water (or almond milk) to a boil.
2. Add ½ cup chopped oats and reduce heat to low. Simmer, stirring occasionally, for about 5 to 7 minutes until the liquid is absorbed and the oats are tender.
3. Once the oats are cooked, add 1 tablespoon ground flax seed, 1 tablespoon chia seeds (if using), and a pinch of salt (optional).
4. Add ½ teaspoon cinnamon and ¼ teaspoon vanilla extract for flavor.
5. Divide the cooked oats between two bowls, and garnish each serving with chopped mixed nuts and fresh or frozen berries.
6. Sprinkle with unsweetened coconut flakes, if desired.
7. If you prefer a sweeter taste, add a small amount of low-glycemic sweetener, such as stevia or monk fruit, or use 1 teaspoon of honey or maple syrup.
8. Stir well and enjoy your healthy, high-fiber cereal today!

Variants and substitutions:

If you want to increase the protein content, add a scoop of unflavored or vanilla protein powder after cooking the oats. Alternatively, add Greek yogurt as a garnish. If you don't have fresh berries, use frozen berries, unsweetened applesauce, or chopped apples or pears. Berries are low in sugar and have a minimal impact on blood sugar levels, making them ideal for diabetics.

Nutritional information (per serving): Calories: 320 kcal; Protein: 10g; Net carbs: 40g; Fiber: 15g; Fat: 15g; Sugars: 6g; Cholesterol 0g; Sodium 50mg; Potassium: 420mg.

Oatmeal with Cinnamon and Berries

Time: *5 min* ***Cook:*** *10 min* ***Servings****: 2*

Ingredients:

- Old-fashioned oatmeal: 1 cup
- Water or unsweetened almond milk: 2 cups (or use skim milk for a creamier option)
- Ground cinnamon: ½ teaspoon
- Fresh or frozen berries: ½ cup (such as blueberries, raspberries, or strawberries)
- Ground flax Seed: 1 tbsp (optional, for added fiber and omega-3s)
- Chopped nuts: 2 tbsp (such as almonds, walnuts, or pecans)
- Vanilla extract: ¼ tsp (optional)
- Salt: pinch (optional)
- Sweetener (optional): stevia, monk fruit, or a drizzle of honey/maple syrup (optional and diabetic-friendly)
- Chia seeds: 1 tbsp (optional, for added fiber)

Instructions:

1. In a medium saucepan, bring 2 cups water (or unsweetened almond milk) to a boil.
2. Add 1 cup rolled oats and reduce heat to low. Simmer oats for about 10 to 15 minutes, stirring occasionally, until oats are soft and have absorbed most of the liquid.
3. Once oats are cooked, stir in ½ teaspoon cinnamon, a pinch of salt (optional), and ¼ teaspoon vanilla extract (if using).
4. Divide cooked oats between two bowls, and garnish each serving with ¼ cup fresh or frozen berries, 1 tablespoon chopped walnuts, and 1 tablespoon ground flax Seed (if using). You can also add chia seeds for an extra boost of fiber.
5. For an extra touch of sweetness, use a drizzle of a diabetic-friendly sweetener, such as stevia or monk fruit. Avoid using too much honey or maple syrup if you are managing your blood sugar levels.
6. Serve the oats warm and enjoy a heart-healthy, high-fiber breakfast!

Variants and substitutions:

If you're short on time, use quick oats, which cook in about 5 minutes. However, rolled oats are better for slower digestion and a lower glycemic impact. Add a tablespoon of Greek yogurt or a scoop of protein powder after cooking to increase the protein content. If you have a nut allergy or want a nut-free version, simply omit the nuts or replace them with seeds like sunflower seeds or pumpkin seeds.

Nutritional information (per serving): Calories: 310 kcal; Protein: 8 g; Net Carbs: 46g; Fiber: 11g; Fat: 12g; Sugar: 6 g (natural sugars from berries); Cholesterol 0g; Sodium 50mg; Potassium: 380mg.

Spinach Smoothie

Time: *5 min* ***Servings****: 2*

Ingredients:

- Fresh spinach: 2 cups (unpressed)
- Unsweetened almond milk: 1 cup (or other unsweetened plant-based milk)
- Greek yogurt (plain, unsweetened, low-fat): ½ cup (adds creaminess and protein)
- Frozen or fresh avocado: ½ medium (adds healthy fats and creaminess)
- Frozen mixed berries: ½ cup (such as blueberries, raspberries, or strawberries)
- Chia seeds: 1 tbsp (for fiber and omega-3s)
- Ground cinnamon: ¼ teaspoon (adds flavor and can help control blood sugar)
- Vanilla extract: ½ tsp (optional for added flavor)
- Stevia or monk fruit sweetener: to taste (optional for extra sweetness)

Instructions:

1. Wash the fresh spinach and make sure the fresh fruit is clean.
2. If you use fresh berries, you can add a couple of ice cubes to the blender for a colder smoothie.
3. In a high-speed blender, combine 2 cups of spinach, 1 cup of unsweetened almond milk, ½ cup of Greek yogurt, ½ avocado, ½ cup of frozen berries, 1 tablespoon of chia seeds, ¼ teaspoon of cinnamon, and ½ teaspoon of vanilla extract (optional).
4. Blend until smooth and creamy. If the smoothie is too thick, add more almond milk a little at a time until you reach your desired consistency.
5. Taste the smoothie. If you like it sweeter, add a few drops of stevia or monk fruit sweetener, which are low-glycemic sweeteners suitable for diabetes.
6. Pour the smoothie into two glasses and serve immediately.

Variants and substitutions:

To increase the protein content, add a scoop of unsweetened protein powder (like whey or plant-based protein) or more Greek yogurt. If you don't have berries, substitute other low-sugar fruits like kiwi, green apple, or cucumber for a different flavor profile. You can prep all the ingredients (except the almond milk) and freeze them in individual smoothie bags. When you're ready to blend, simply add the almond milk and blend.

Nutritional information (per serving): Calories: 184 kcal; Protein: 9g; Net Carbs: 17g; Fiber: 10g; Fat: 5g; Sugar: 6 g (from natural sugars present in fruit and yogurt); Cholesterol 0g; Sodium 150mg; Potassium: 620 mg (helps regulate blood pressure).

Greek Yogurt Parfait

Time: *5 min* **Servings**: 2

Ingredients:

- Greek yogurt (plain, unsweetened, low-fat): 1 ½ cups
- Fresh berries (e.g., blueberries, raspberries, strawberries): 1 cup
- Chia seeds: 1 tbsp (optional, for extra fiber and omega-3s)
- Unsweetened granola (low sugar, whole grain): ¼ cup
- Ground cinnamon: ¼ tsp (optional, helps control blood sugar)
- Vanilla extract: ½ tsp (optional for flavor)
- Almonds or walnuts (chopped): 2 tbsp (for crunch and healthy fats)
- Stevia or monk fruit sweetener: to taste (optional, if you prefer a sweeter flavor)
- Unsweetened coconut flakes: 1 tbsp (optional, for a stronger flavor)

Instructions:

1. In a small bowl, combine 1 ½ cups plain Greek yogurt with ½ teaspoon vanilla extract (optional) and a sprinkle of ground cinnamon. Stir until smooth. Taste the yogurt, and add a little more stevia or monk fruit sweetener if you like it sweeter.
2. Divide the yogurt mixture evenly between two glasses or serving bowls, and top each serving with ½ cup fresh berries.
3. Sprinkle each parfait with 1 tablespoon chia seeds, 2 tablespoons unsweetened granola, and 1 tablespoon chopped nuts (almonds or walnuts).
4. For added texture and flavor, garnish with unsweetened coconut flakes, if desired.
5. Serve the parfait immediately or refrigerate for up to 30 minutes if you prefer it slightly chilled.

Variants and substitutions:

Use any low-glycemic fruit you like. Berries are great for managing blood sugar levels, but you can also try kiwi, green apple, or a small amount of diced peaches. If you are sensitive to dairy or want a plant-based option, use unsweetened coconut yogurt or almond milk yogurt instead of Greek yogurt. You can make these parfaits the night before. Just keep the granola separate until ready to serve so it stays crunchy.

Nutritional information (per serving): Calories: 240 kcal; Protein: 16g; Net Carbs: 22g; Fiber: 4g; Fat: 10g; Sugar: 9 g (from natural sugars found in berries and yogurt); Cholesterol 0g; Sodium 75mg; Potassium: 350 mg (good for regulating blood pressure).

Avocado Toast with Eggs

Time: *10 min* ***Cook:*** *5 min* ***Servings****: 2*

Ingredients:

- Whole-grain or multigrain bread: 4 slices
- Avocado: 1 large, ripe
- Lemon juice: 1 tbsp (optional, for freshness and flavor)
- Eggs: 2 large
- Olive oil or cooking spray: 1 tsp (for cooking eggs)
- Cracked black pepper: to taste
- Sea salt: to taste (optional, for low-sodium diets, limit or omit)
- Red chili flakes: ¼ tsp (optional, for a spicy kick)
- Fresh herbs (such as parsley or cilantro): 1 tbsp, chopped (optional)
- Chia seeds or hemp seeds: 1 tbsp (optional, for extra fiber and omega-3s)

Instructions:

1. Halve the avocado, remove the pit, and scoop the flesh into a small bowl, and mash it with a fork until smooth but still slightly lumpy.
2. Add 1 tablespoon lemon juice, a pinch of sea salt (if using), and ground black pepper to taste. Mix well and set aside.
3. While you prepare the avocado, toast the whole wheat bread slices in a toaster oven until golden and crispy.
4. Heat a nonstick skillet over medium heat and lightly coat with olive oil or cooking spray.
5. Crack the eggs into the skillet and cook them however you like: sunny-side up, fried, or scrambled. For a poached version, you can cook the eggs in boiling water with a splash of vinegar.
6. Season the eggs with a little salt (optional) and pepper to taste.
7. Spread the mashed avocado mixture evenly over the toasted bread slices.
8. Place an egg on each slice of avocado toast, and for added flavor, sprinkle with red chili flakes, fresh herbs, and chia seeds (or hemp seeds), if desired.
9. Serve the avocado toast immediately. Optionally, garnish with a squeeze of extra lemon juice or a drizzle of extra virgin olive oil for added flavor.

Variants and substitutions:

If you're trying to lower your cholesterol or eat a plant-based diet, replace the eggs with scrambled tofu or a vegan egg substitute. Choose a low-glycemic bread like whole wheat, multigrain, or sprouted grains for better blood sugar control. Avoid white bread or highly processed varieties. Pair your toast with a side of fresh vegetables or a simple salad to add more veggies and increase the fiber content of your meal.

Nutritional information (per serving): Calories: 260 kcal; Protein: 13g; Net Carbs: 12g; Fiber: 6g; Fat: 21g; Sugar: 260mg (varies with bread and salt usage); Cholesterol 0,2g; Sodium 0,2g; 700mg (thanks to avocado and eggs).

Veggie Omelet

Time: *10 min* ***Cook:*** *10 min* ***Servings****: 2*

Ingredients:

- Eggs: 4 large
- Peppers: ½ cup, diced (any color)
- Spinach: ½ cup, fresh
- Mushrooms: ½ cup, sliced
- Red onion: ¼ cup, diced
- Olive oil: 1 tsp (or use nonstick spray)
- Skim milk: 2 tbsp (optional, for fluffier eggs)
- Ground black pepper: to taste
- Sea salt: optional, to taste (low sodium is recommended)
- Fresh herbs: 1 tbsp, chopped (for example, parsley, cilantro, or chives)
- Cheese: 2 tbsp grated low-fat cheese (optional, use feta or cheddar)
- Chili flakes: optional, for a spicy kick

Instructions:

1. Wash and dice the bell peppers, slice the mushrooms, dice the red onion, and rinse the spinach, and add them to a preheated nonstick skillet over medium heat with 1 teaspoon of olive oil. Cook until softened (about 3-4 minutes).
2. Add the spinach and cook for another 1-2 minutes, until wilted. Set the greens aside on a plate.
3. In a medium bowl, whisk together the eggs, milk (if using), pepper, and a pinch of salt (optional).
4. Heat another skillet with a light coating of oil or nonstick spray, pour in half of the egg mixture, and cook over medium heat until the eggs are set around the edges but still slightly soft in the center (about 2-3 minutes).
5. Add half of the sauteed vegetables to one side of the omelet.
6. Sprinkle 1 tablespoon of cheese (optional) over the vegetables.
7. Fold the omelet in half and cook for another minute or until the eggs are cooked through.
8. Slide the omelet onto a plate and repeat the process for the second omelet.
9. Garnish with fresh herbs and an optional sprinkle of chili flakes.

Variants and substitutions:

Use egg whites or an egg substitute to reduce the cholesterol and fat content. To do this, substitute 8 egg whites for the 4 whole eggs. Replace the eggs with a plant-based egg alternative (like JUST Egg) and use dairy-free cheese. Add cooked chicken, turkey, or tofu to increase the protein content of the dish.

Nutritional information (per serving): Calories: 180 kcal: Protein: 14 g; Net Carbs: 7 g; Fiber: 2 g; Sugars: 3 g; Fat: 11 g; Saturated fat: 3 g; Cholesterol: 340 mg; Sodium: 210 mg (varies based on use of cheese and salt); Potassium: 400 mg.

Almond Flour Pancakes

Time: *10 min* ***Cook:*** *15 min* ***Servings****: 2*

Ingredients:

- Almond flour: 1 cup
- Eggs: 2 large
- Unsweetened almond milk: ¼ cup (or other non-dairy milk)
- Baking powder: ½ tsp
- Vanilla extract: 1 tsp
- Ground cinnamon: ¼ tsp (optional)
- Salt: pinch
- Olive or coconut oil: 1 tsp for cooking (or nonstick spray)
- Fresh berries: for garnish (optional)
- Sugar-free syrup or plain Greek yogurt: for serving (optional)

Instructions:

1. In a medium bowl, whisk together the eggs, unsweetened almond milk, and vanilla extract until smooth.
2. In a separate bowl, whisk together the almond flour, baking powder, cinnamon (if using), and salt.
3. Gradually add the dry ingredients to the wet ingredients, stirring until well combined and the batter is smooth.
4. Heat a nonstick skillet or griddle over medium heat and lightly grease with olive oil or coconut oil. Pour about 2 tablespoons of batter into the skillet for each pancake, spreading it out slightly with the back of a spoon. (Almond flour pancakes will be slightly thicker than regular pancakes.)
5. Cook for about 2-3 minutes, or until bubbles form on the top and the edges begin to set.
6. Carefully flip the pancakes and cook for another 1-2 minutes, until golden brown and cooked through. 4. Serve:
7. Serve the pancakes warm, garnished with fresh berries, a drizzle of sugar-free syrup or a spoonful of plain Greek yogurt for extra creaminess and protein.

Variants and substitutions:

Use unsweetened coconut milk or oat milk instead of almond milk. For extra sweetness, add monk fruit or stevia to taste (both are diabetic friendly). Add a tablespoon of lemon zest or a pinch of nutmeg for a more complex flavor.

Nutritional information (per serving): Calories: 300 kcal; Protein: 12g; Net Carbs: 5g; Fiber: 4g; Fat: 57g; Sugar: 2g; Cholesterol 185mg; Sodium 190mg; Potassium: 150mg.

Chia Seed Pudding

Time: *10 min* ***Servings****: 2*

Ingredients:

- Chia seeds: ¼ cup
- Unsweetened almond milk: 1 cup (or any other unsweetened plant-based milk)
- Vanilla extract: ½ tsp
- Cinnamon powder: ¼ tsp
- Sweetener (optional): 1-2 tsp stevia, monk fruit, or erythritol (all diabetic-friendly sweeteners)
- Fresh berries: ¼ cup for topping (optional)
- Unsweetened shredded coconut: 1 tbsp for topping (optional)
- Chopped nuts: 1 tbsp (optional; almonds or walnuts are good choices)

Instructions:

1. In a small bowl or glass jar, combine the chia seeds, unsweetened almond milk, vanilla extract, ground cinnamon, and your favorite sweetener (if using).
2. Stir the mixture well to ensure the chia seeds are evenly distributed throughout the liquid.
3. Let the mixture sit for 5 minutes, then stir again to break up any clumps of chia seeds that may have formed.
4. Cover the bowl or jar and refrigerate for at least 30-45 minutes, or overnight if making ahead. This allows the chia seeds to absorb the liquid and thicken, creating a pudding-like consistency.
5. Once the chia pudding has thickened, give it one last stir.
6. Divide the pudding into two portions and garnish with fresh berries, unsweetened shredded coconut, and/or chopped walnuts for added texture and flavor (optional).

Variants and substitutions:

You can use coconut milk, oat milk, or soy milk in place of almond milk. Just be sure to choose unsweetened varieties to keep the carbs count low. For extra protein, add a tablespoon of unsweetened Greek yogurt or a scoop of vanilla-flavored protein powder. Try adding a pinch of nutmeg, cardamom, or pumpkin spice for a warming flavor profile.

Nutritional information (per serving): Calories: 160 kcal; Protein: 5g; Carbohydrates: 12g; Fiber: 10g; Sugars: 1g (from natural sources); Fat: 9g; Saturated fat: 0.5g; Sodium: 125mg; Potassium: 200mg; Net carbohydrates: 2g

Spinach and Feta Breakfast Wrap

Time: *10 min* ***Cook:*** *10 min* ***Servings****: 2*

Ingredients:

- Olive oil (optional): 1 tsp (or use cooking spray)
- Eggs: 4 large (or egg whites to lower cholesterol)
- Fresh spinach: 2 cups (coarsely chopped)
- Feta cheese: ¼ cup (crumbled, low-fat or regular)
- Whole wheat tortillas: 2 medium (low-carbs or high-fiber, if desired)
- Garlic powder: ¼ tsp (optional)
- Black pepper: to taste
- Piece tomatoes: ¼ cup (halved, for extra freshness)
- Avocado slices: ½ avocado (optional, for added healthy fat)
- Fresh herbs: A few sprigs of parsley or cilantro for garnish (optional)

Instructions:

1. In a medium bowl, crack the 4 eggs and beat until smooth. If you prefer to reduce the fat, you can use egg whites or a mix of whole eggs and egg whites. Season with a pinch of garlic powder (optional) and black pepper to taste.
2. Heat a nonstick skillet over medium heat. Add 1 teaspoon of olive oil (or use cooking spray for a lower-fat version), and once hot, add the chopped spinach and saute for 1-2 minutes until wilted.
3. Remove the spinach from the skillet and set aside.
4. Pour the beaten eggs into the same skillet and cook over medium heat. Stir occasionally with a spatula to scramble the eggs, cooking until set (about 3-4 minutes). Avoid overcooking to keep them soft.
5. Once the eggs are cooked, add the sauteed spinach and crumbled feta cheese. Mix until smooth.
6. Microwave whole wheat tortillas for about 15-20 seconds to make them more pliable.
7. Divide the egg, spinach and feta mixture between the two tortillas.
8. Add halved cherry tomatoes and avocado slices on top (optional, but highly recommended for extra flavor and nutrition).
9. Roll the tortilla into a wrap, folding the sides first and then rolling from the bottom. Halve, if desired, and serve warm.

Variants and substitutions:

Add lean protein like grilled chicken or sliced turkey to the wrap for added protein. Swap the eggs for scrambled tofu and the feta for a vegan cheese, or simply leave out the cheese for a plant-based version.

Nutritional information (per serving): Calories: 320 kcal; Protein: 19g; Net Carbs: 15g; Fiber: 3g; Fat: 21g; Sugar: 3g (natural sugars from vegetables)g; Cholesterol 275mg (or less if using egg whites); Sodium 500mg (can be reduced with low sodium feta).

Grilled Chiken and Vegetable Skewers

Time: *15 min* ***Cook:*** *20 min* ***Servings****: 2*

Ingredients:

- Chicken breasts: 2 skinless and boneless (8 ounces each)
- Peppers: 1 medium (any color, chopped)
- Zucchini: 1 small (thickly sliced)
- Red onion: 1 small (chopped)
- Pink tomatoes: 8-10 (whole)
- Olive oil: 2 tablespoons
- Lemon juice: 2 tbsp
- Garlic powder: ½ tsp
- Dried oregano: ½ tsp
- Ground cumin: ½ tap
- Black pepper: to taste
- Salt: ¼ tap (optional, or use low-sodium)
- Fresh parsley: for garnish (optional)

Instructions:

1. Cut the chicken breasts into cubes (about 1 inch) and place in a bowl.
2. In a small bowl, mix together the olive oil, lemon juice, garlic powder, oregano, cumin, black pepper, and a pinch of salt (optional). Whisk until combined.
3. Pour the marinade over the chicken, toss to coat well, and let sit for at least 10 minutes while you prep the vegetables. If you have extra time, you can marinate the chicken for up to 2 hours in the refrigerator for extra flavor.
4. Chop the peppers, zucchini, and red onion into small pieces, and leave the cherry tomatoes whole, and toss them in a little olive oil and season with a pinch of salt and black pepper.
5. If using wooden skewers, soak them in water for about 15 minutes to prevent them from burning on the grill. Thread the marinated chicken and vegetables onto skewers, alternating chicken, bell peppers, zucchini, red onion, and cherry tomatoes.
6. Preheat the grill (or grill pan) to medium-high heat, and arrange the skewers, and cook for 10 to 15 minutes, turning them on each side to ensure even cooking. The chicken should be cooked through.
7. Remove the skewers from the grill and let them rest for a few minutes before serving.
8. Serve the skewers hot, garnished with chopped fresh parsley for extra freshness.

Variants and substitutions:

Replace the chicken with extra-firm tofu or tempeh cubes. Marinate and grill them the same way as the chicken. Feel free to add other vegetables like mushrooms, yellow squash, or eggplant for more variety.

Nutritional information (per serving): Calories: 350 kcal; Protein: 32g; Net Carbs: 9g; Fiber: 4g; Fat: 2g; Sugar: 0; Cholesterol 90mg; Sodium 250mg.

Lentil Soup with Spinach and Tomatoes

Time: *10 min* ***Cook:*** *30 min* ***Servings****: 2*

Ingredients:

- Olive oil: 1 tbsp
- Onion: 1 small, finely chopped
- Garlic: 2 cloves, minced
- Carrot: 1 medium, diced
- Celery: 1 stalk, diced
- Canned tomatoes, diced: 1 cup (preferably low-sodium)
- Dried lentils: ½ cup, rinsed (green or brown)
- Vegetable broth: 3 cups (low-sodium)
- Ground cumin: ½ tsp
- Paprika: ½ tsp
- Dried thyme: ½ tsp
- Baby spinach: 2 cups (fresh)
- Salt: to taste (optional, use sparingly or low-sodium)
- Black pepper: to taste
- Lemon juice: 1 tbsp (optional, for brightness)
- Fresh parsley: 1 tbsp, chopped (optional for garnish)

Instructions:

1. Heat the olive oil in a medium saucepan over medium heat, and add the onion, carrot, and celery and saute for about 5 minutes until softened.
2. Add the garlic and cook for another minute until fragrant, but be careful not to burn it.
3. Add the lentils, cumin, paprika, and thyme. Cook for 1-2 minutes, allowing the lentils and spices to mix well with the aromatics.
4. Add the diced tomatoes and vegetable stock. Stir to combine, then bring the mixture to a boil.
5. Once boiling, reduce the heat to low and cover. Let the soup cook for 20-25 minutes, or until the lentils are tender but not mushy. Stir occasionally.
6. Add the baby spinach and let it wilt for 2-3 minutes.
7. Add salt (optional) and black pepper to taste. If desired, add a squeeze of lemon juice for a zing.
8. Divide the soup into bowls, garnish with fresh parsley and serve hot.

Variants and substitutions:

You can add other non-starchy vegetables like zucchini, mushrooms, or kale to increase the fiber content. For a little heat, add a pinch of red pepper flakes or a pinch of cayenne pepper. Swap the spinach for Swiss chard or kale for a heartier texture.

Nutritional information (per serving): Calories: 280 kcal; Fats: 6g; Proteins: 19g; Net Carbs: 24g; Fibers: 12g; Sugars: 8g (from vegetables); Cholesterol 0g; Sodium 250mg.

Baked Salmon with Asparagus

Time: *10 min* ***Cook:*** *25 min* ***Servings****: 4*

Ingredients:

- Salmon Fillets: 4 fillets (6 ounces each)
- Asparagus: 1 pound (trimmed)
- Olive Oil: 3 tbsp
- Garlic: 3 cloves, minced
- Lemon: 1 (zest and juice)
- Dijon Mustard: 2 tsp
- Fresh Parsley: 2 tbsp, minced (optional)
- Black Pepper: to taste
- Salt: to taste (optional or use low sodium)
- Dried Thyme: 1 tsp
- Red Chili Flakes: optional, for a little heat

Instructions:

1. Set the oven temperature to 400°F (200°C).
2. Snip off the tough ends of the asparagus (about 1-2 inches from the bottom), and
3. place them on a parchment-lined baking sheet.
4. Drizzle the asparagus with 1 tablespoon of the olive oil, season with a pinch of salt (optional), pepper, and half the minced garlic. Toss to coat the asparagus evenly.
5. Arrange the salmon fillets on the same baking sheet, leaving room between the fillets and the asparagus.
6. In a small bowl, combine 2 tablespoons of the olive oil, lemon zest, lemon juice, Dijon mustard, remaining garlic, thyme, black pepper, and a pinch of salt (if desired).
7. Brush this lemon-garlic mixture over the tops of the salmon fillets.
8. Place the pan in the preheated oven and bake for 12 to 15 minutes, or until the salmon is opaque and flakes easily with a fork, and the asparagus is tender but crisp.
9. Once baked, garnish the salmon with fresh parsley and the remaining lemon juice.

Variants and substitutions:

Replace the asparagus with other non-starchy vegetables like broccoli, green beans, or zucchini. These vegetables can be roasted alongside the salmon for a similar cooking time. Add a topping of chopped almonds or walnuts over the salmon fillets for added texture and healthy fats. You can replace the salmon with trout, cod, or another fatty fish that provides heart-healthy omega-3s.

Nutritional information (per serving): Calories: 360 kcal; Protein: 12g; Net Carbs: 3g; Fiber: 17g; Fat: 16g; Sugar: 3g; Cholesterol 0g; Sodium 120 mg (may be less with reduced salt intake).

Broccoli and Chicken Stir-Fry

Time: *15 min* ***Cook:*** *20 min* ***Servings****: 4*

Ingredients:

- Chicken breast (boneless, skinless): 1 pound, thinly sliced
- Broccoli florets: 4 cups (about 1 large head)
- Red bell pepper: 1, thinly sliced
- Carrot: 1 medium, thinly sliced or julienned
- Garlic: 3 cloves, minced
- Ginger: 1-inch piece, minced or grated
- Low-sodium soy sauce: ¼ cup
- Rice vinegar: 1 tbsp
- Sesame oil: 1 tbsp
- Olive oil: 1 tbsp
- Cornstarch: 1 tbsp (for thickening)
- Water: ¼ cup (for sauce)
- Black pepper: to taste
- Sesame seeds: 1 tbsp (optional, for garnish)
- Cooked brown rice: for serving (optional)

Instructions:

1. Slice the chicken breast into thin strips and season with a little black pepper. Set aside while you prepare the vegetables.
2. In a small bowl, whisk together the low-sodium soy sauce, rice vinegar, sesame oil, and cornstarch mixed with water (to thicken the sauce). Set this sauce aside.
3. Heat the olive oil in a large skillet or wok over medium-high heat, and add the chicken strips, cooking for 5-7 minutes, until golden brown and cooked through. Stir occasionally to ensure even cooking. Once cooked, remove the chicken from the pan and set aside.
4. In the same skillet, add a little more olive oil if needed. Add the broccoli florets, bell pepper, carrot, garlic, and ginger, and saute for 5-6 minutes, until the vegetables are tender but still crunchy. You can add 1-2 tablespoons of water to the pan to help steam the broccoli if needed.
5. Return the cooked chicken to the pan with the vegetables.
6. Pour in the prepared soy sauce mixture and stir well to coat all the ingredients. Cook for another 2-3 minutes until the sauce has thickened slightly and everything is hot.
7. Garnish with sesame seeds (optional) and serve the stir-fry over cooked brown rice or enjoy on its own for a low-carb option.

Variants and substitutions:

Swap the chicken for tofu or shrimp for a vegetarian or pescatarian version. You can add other non-starchy vegetables like snap peas, zucchini, or mushrooms depending on what you have on hand. Add a pinch of red pepper flakes or sriracha for a little spiciness.

Nutritional information (per serving): Calories: 20 kcal; Protein: 30g; Net Carbs: 9g; Fiber: 7g; Fat: 12g; Sugar: 7g; Cholesterol 65mg; Sodium 380mg (using low-sodium soy sauce).

Spicy Grilled Shrimp and Vegetable Skewers

Time: *15 min* ***Cook:*** *15 min* ***Servings****: 4*

Ingredients:

- Shrimp: 1 pound, large, peeled and gutted
- Zucchini: 2 medium, sliced
- Red bell pepper: 1 large, chopped
- Red onion: 1 medium, chopped
- Cherries: 1 cup
- Olive oil: 2 tbsp
- Lemon juice: 2 tbsp (freshly squeezed)
- Garlic: 3 cloves, minced
- Smoked paprika: 1 tsp
- Cayenne pepper: ½ tsp (adjust for spiciness)
- Cumin: ½ tsp
- Dried oregano: 1 tsp
- Cracked black pepper: to taste
- Salt: to taste (optional, or use a low-sodium alternative)
- Fresh cilantro or parsley: for garnish
- Skewers: soaked metal or wooden skewers

Instructions:

1. In a large bowl, whisk together the olive oil, lemon juice, minced garlic, smoked paprika, cayenne, cumin, oregano, black pepper, and a pinch of salt (if using). Taste the marinade and adjust the spiciness to your liking, adding more cayenne if needed.
2. Add the shrimp to the bowl and toss to coat evenly with the marinade. Cover and let marinate in the refrigerator for 10 to 15 minutes while you prepare the vegetables.
3. Slice the zucchini into rounds, dice the red bell pepper and onion, and set the cherry tomatoes aside and toss in a separate bowl with a drizzle of olive oil and a pinch of black pepper. You can add a pinch of the leftover marinade for extra flavor.
4. Thread the shrimp and vegetables onto skewers, alternating shrimp, zucchini slices, bell peppers, onion pieces, and cherry tomatoes.
5. Preheat the grill to medium-high heat (about 400°F) or heat a grill pan on the stove.
6. Place the skewers on the grill and cook for 2 to 3 minutes per side or until the shrimp are pink and opaque and the vegetables are slightly charred but tender. Be careful not to overcook the shrimp.
7. Once cooked, remove the skewers from the grill and sprinkle with fresh cilantro or parsley for garnish.
8. Serve immediately with a salad, quinoa, or brown rice for a heartier meal.

Variants and substitutions:

You can substitute the shrimp with chicken breast pieces or tofu for a different source of protein. Adjust the cooking time accordingly (chicken will take longer to cook than shrimp).

Nutritional information (per serving): Calories: 220 kcal; Protein: 22g; Net Carbs: 48g; Fiber: 23g; Fat: 29g; Sugar: 12g: Cholesterol 160mg; Sodium 200mg.

Grilled Salmon with Cucumber Salad

Time: *15 min* ***Cook:*** *15 min* ***Servings****: 4*

Ingredients:

For the salmon:

- Salmon fillets: 4 (about 5-6 ounces each)
- Olive oil: 2 tbsp
- Garlic: 3 cloves, minced
- Lemon juice: 2 tbsp
- Dijon mustard: 1 tbsp
- Dried dill: 1 tsp (or fresh dill, minced)
- Crunk black pepper: to taste
- Salt: to taste (optional, or use a low-sodium alternative)

For the cucumber salad:

- Cucumber: 2 large cucumbers, thinly sliced
- Red onion: ½ small, thinly sliced
- Fresh dill: 2 tbsp, minced
- Greek yogurt: ¼ cup (plain, unsweetened)
- Lemon juice: 1 tbsp
- Olive oil: 1 tbsp
- Crunk black pepper: to taste
- Salt: to taste (optional)

Instructions:

1. In a small bowl, whisk together the olive oil, minced garlic, lemon juice, Dijon mustard, dried dill, black pepper, and a pinch of salt (if using).
2. Rub the salmon fillets with the marinade, making sure they are evenly coated. Let them marinate for 10 to 15 minutes while you prepare the cucumber salad.
3. In a large bowl, combine the cucumber slices, red onion, and fresh dill.
4. In another small bowl, whisk together the Greek yogurt, lemon juice, olive oil, black pepper, and a pinch of salt. Pour the dressing over the cucumber mixture and toss gently until everything is well coated. Chill the salad in the refrigerator while you grill the salmon.
5. Preheat the grill or broiler pan to medium-high heat (about 375°F - 400°F). Once hot, place the marinated salmon fillets skin-side down on the grill. Grill for 4-5 minutes per side, or until the salmon is cooked through and flakes easily with a fork.
6. For added flavor, squeeze a little fresh lemon juice over the salmon as it grills.
7. Once cooked, transfer the salmon fillets to a serving platter. Serve each grilled salmon fillet with a generous portion of cucumber salad on the side.
8. Garnish with extra lemon wedges and a sprinkle of fresh parsley or dill for added freshness.

Variants and substitutions:

If you don't have salmon, you can substitute other fatty fish like trout or mackerel. For a vegetarian option, grilled tofu or portobello mushrooms would work well.

Nutritional information (per serving): Calories: 320 kcal; Protein: 27g; Net Carbs: 6g; Fiber: 1g; Fat: 21g; Sugar: 2g; Cholesterol: 070mg; Sodium: 200mg.

Zucchini Noodles with Tomato Sauce

Time: *10 min* ***Cook:*** *15 min* ***Servings****: 4*

Ingredients:

- *For the zucchini noodles:*
- Squash: 4 medium zucchini, spiralized into noodles (about 5-6 cups)
- Olive oil: 1 tbsp
- Garlic: 2 cloves, minced
- Salt: a pinch
- Black pepper: to taste
- *For the tomato sauce:*
- Olive oil: 1 tbsp
- Onion: 1 small onion, finely chopped
- Garlic: 3 cloves, minced
- Canned crushed tomatoes: 1 can (14 oz, no sugar added)
- Tomato paste: 1 tbsp
- Dried oregano: 1 tsp
- Dried basil: 1 tsp (or 2 tablespoons fresh basil, minced)
- Crushed red pepper flakes: ¼ teaspoon (optional, for spice)
- Salt: to taste (optional, or use a low-sodium option)
- Black pepper: to taste
- Parsley or fresh basil: for garnish

Instructions:

1. Using a spiralizer, spiralize the zucchini into spaghetti-like shapes, alternatively you can use a julienne peeler or purchase pre-spiralized zucchini from the supermarket.
2. Place the spiralized zucchini on a clean dish towel and sprinkle lightly with salt. Let sit for about 10 minutes to help remove excess moisture. Then, gently pat the spaghetti dry with the towel.
3. In a large skillet, heat 1 tbsp of olive oil over medium heat, add the onion, and cook until softened, about 5 minutes. Then add the garlic and cook for another 30 seconds.
4. Add the crushed tomatoes, tomato paste, oregano, basil, and red pepper flakes (if using). Season with a pinch of salt and black pepper to taste.
5. Bring the sauce to a boil and cook for 10-15 minutes, stirring occasionally, until slightly thickened. If the sauce becomes too thick, add a splash of water or vegetable broth. Taste and adjust salt if necessary.
6. In a separate large skillet, heat 1 tbsp of the olive oil over medium heat, and add the zucchini noodles and minced garlic. Sauté for about 2-3 minutes, stirring often, until the noodles are tender but still slightly firm (al dente). Avoid overcooking them, as they may become too soft and watery. Season with a pinch of black pepper and salt (optional).
7. Distribute the zucchini noodles evenly among 4 plates, and drizzle with the homemade tomato sauce and garnish with parsley or basil.

Variants and substitutions:

Keep it plant-based by skipping the parmesan or substituting with nutritional yeast for a cheesy, vegan flavor.

Nutritional information (per serving): Calories: 140 kcal; Protein: 4g; Net Carbs: 10g; Fiber: 4g; Fat: 16g; Sugar: 10g (from tomatoes and courgettes); Cholesterol 0g; Sodium 160mg.

Cauliflower Fried Rice

Time: *10 min* ***Cook:*** *20 min* ***Servings****: 4*

Ingredients:

- Cauliflower: 1 medium head, grated or finely chopped (or use 4 cups pre-riced cauliflower)
- Olive oil: 2 tbsp
- Onion: 1 small, finely chopped
- Garlic: 3 cloves, minced
- Carrots: 1 medium, diced
- Peas: ½ cup (frozen or fresh)
- Bell pepper: 1 small, diced (optional)
- Eggs: 2 large
- Low-sodium soy sauce: 2-3 tbsp (or tamari for gluten-free)
- Sesame oil: 1 tsp (optional, for flavor)
- Green onions: 2, chopped
- Salt and pepper: to taste
- Fresh cilantro: for garnish (optional)
- Sriracha or hot sauce: for serving (optional)

Instructions:

1. If you're using a whole head of cauliflower, cut it into large florets and pulse until it resembles grains of rice. If you don't have a food processor, you can finely chop the cauliflower by hand or use a box grater. If you're using store-bought riced cauliflower, make sure it's fresh or thawed if frozen.
2. Heat 1 tablespoon of olive oil in a large skillet or wok over medium heat, add the onion and saue for about 3-4 minutes until softened, then add the garlic, carrots, peas, and bell pepper (if using). Cook for another 5-7 minutes, stirring occasionally, until the vegetables are tender. Season lightly with salt and a sprinkle of pepper.
3. Push the vegetables to one side of the pan and add 1 teaspoon of olive oil to the empty space. Crack the eggs into the skillet and scramble, stirring until cooked through (about 2-3 minutes). Once cooked, toss the scrambled eggs with the vegetables.
4. Add the cauliflower rice to the skillet and toss everything together.
5. Cook for 5-7 minutes, stirring occasionally, until the cauliflower is tender but not mushy.
6. Mix together the low-sodium soy sauce (or tamari for gluten-free) and sesame oil (if using). Adjust the seasoning by adding more soy sauce or a pinch of salt, if needed.
7. Add the chopped scallions and any optional protein, such as cooked chicken, shrimp, or tofu. Cook for another 1-2 minutes to heat through.
8. Divide among 4 bowls, and garnish with fresh cilantro and drizzle with sriracha or hot sauce for a little heat, if desired.

Variants and substitutions:

For a plant-based meal, use cubed tofu or edamame for added protein. Add a splash of rice vinegar or lime juice for brightness.

Nutritional information (per serving): Calories: 170 kcal; Protein: 7g; Net Carbs: 8g; Fiber: 10g; Fat: 9g; Sugar: 8g; Cholesterol 0,2g; Sodium 250mg.

Baked Apple with Cinnamon and Nuts

Time: *10 min* ***Cook:*** *30 min* ***Servings:*** *4*

Ingredients:

- Apples: 4 medium (preferably Granny Smith, Fuji, or Gala for lower sugar content)
- Cinnamon: 1 tsp (ground)
- Chopped nuts: ¼ cup (such as walnuts, pecans, or almonds)
- Unsweetened raisins: 2 tbsp (optional, for natural sweetness)
- Rolled oats: 2 tbsp (optional, for texture and fiber)
- Vanilla extract: ½ tsp
- Unsweetened almond milk: ¼ cup (or other milk alternative)
- Butter or coconut oil: 1 tbsp (optional, for more body)
- Sugar substitute: 1-2 tsp (optional, such as stevia or monk fruit)
- Water: ½ cup

Instructions:

1. Set the oven temperature to 350°F (175°C).
2. Wash and core the apples, leaving the bottoms intact to form a "well" for the filling.
3. Optionally, peel the top halves of the apples if you prefer a softer texture, but the peel provides additional fiber, and arrange them on a baking sheet.
4. In a small bowl, combine the chopped walnuts, ground cinnamon, raisins (if using), rolled oats (optional), and vanilla extract.
5. Add the unsweetened almond milk and optional sugar substitute. If desired, add butter or coconut oil for extra richness. This step is optional but adds a nice depth of flavor.
6. Spoon the nut mixture into the cored apples, gently pressing the filling down. Divide the mixture evenly among the 4 apples.
7. Pour ½ cup of water into the bottom of the pan to loosen the apples and prevent them from drying out. Cover the pan with foil and bake the apples in the preheated oven for 20 minutes.
8. Then remove the foil and bake for another 10 to 15 minutes, or until the apples are fork tender and the filling is golden brown and fragrant.
9. Remove the baked apples from the oven and let them cool slightly before serving. You can enjoy the apples as is, or pair them with a scoop of unsweetened Greek yogurt or a small scoop of unsweetened vanilla ice cream for extra creaminess.

Variants and substitutions:

For those with nut allergies, use sunflower seeds, pumpkin seeds, or toasted coconut flakes instead of nuts. Add a pinch of nutmeg or ginger for a warmer, more intense flavor.

Nutritional information (per serving): Calories: 150 kcal; Protein: 2g; Net Carbs: 20g; Fiber: 12g; Fat: 29g; Sugar: 16g (from the apple, with optional raisins adding more natural sugar); Cholesterol 0g; Sodium 10mg.

Hearty Vegetable Soup

Time: *10 min* ***Cook:*** *35 min* ***Servings****: 4*

Ingredients:

- Olive oil: 1 tbsp (or any heart-healthy oil like avocado oil)
- Yellow onion: 1 medium, chopped
- Garlic: 3 cloves, minced
- Celery: 2 stalks, minced
- Carrots: 2 medium, sliced
- Zucchini: 1 medium, diced
- Bell pepper: 1 medium, diced (red, yellow, or green)
- Tomatoes: 1 can (14.5 ounces), diced, no salt added
- Vegetable broth: 4 cups (low sodium)
- Spinach: 2 cups, fresh or 1 cup frozen
- Cabbage: 1 cup, chopped
- Green beans: 1 cup, fresh or frozen
- Fresh parsley: ¼ cup, chopped (optional)
- Bay leaf: 1
- Dried thyme: 1 tsp
- Dried basil: 1 tsp
- Black pepper: ¼ tsp (or (like to taste)
- Salt: ¼ tsp (optional, use a salt substitute or skip if preferred)

Instructions:

1. In a large saucepan or Dutch oven, heat 1 tablespoon of the olive oil over medium heat, add the chopped onion and garlic and sauté for 2 to 3 minutes, until the onion is soft and translucent.
2. Combine the carrots, celery, zucchini and bell pepper. Cook for about 5 minutes, stirring occasionally, until the vegetables begin to soften.
3. Add the diced tomatoes (with their juices) and vegetable broth. Stir to combine.
4. Mix in the green beans, chopped cabbage and spinach. If using frozen spinach, add it straight from the freezer.
5. Add the bay leaf, dried thyme, dried basil, black pepper and optional salt.
6. Bring the soup to a boil, then reduce the heat to low, cover and simmer for 20 to 25 minutes. Stir occasionally to ensure the vegetables are cooking evenly. Taste and adjust seasoning if necessary.
7. Remove the bay leaf before serving. Ladle the soup into bowls and garnish with fresh parsley if desired.

Variants and substitutions:

For an even lower carbs version, skip the carrots and replace them with more zucchini, mushrooms, or cauliflower.

Nutritional information (per serving): Calories: 120 kcal; Protein: 3g; Net Carbs: 13g; Fiber: 8g; Fat: 1g; Sugar: 7g; Cholesterol 0g; Sodium 240 mg (varies based on broth and salt added).

Stuffed Bell Peppers with Ground Turkey and Quinoa

Time: *15 min* ***Cook:*** *35 min* ***Servings****: 4*

Ingredients:

- Bell peppers: 4 large (red, yellow, or green), tops removed and seeds
- Ground turkey or chicken: 1 pound (lean or substitute ground beef, tofu, or lentils)
- Olive oil: 1 tbsp (for sauteing)
- Onion: 1 medium, finely chopped
- Garlic: 2 cloves, minced
- Cooked quinoa or brown rice: 1 cup (for a low-carbs option, use cauliflower rice)
- Tomato sauce: 1 cup (low sodium)
- Zucchini: 1 small, diced (optional)
- Carrot: 1 small, grated (optional)
- Spinach: 1 cup, chopped (fresh or frozen)
- Cumin: 1 tsp
- Smoked paprika: 1 tsp
- Dried oregano: 1 tsp
- Black pepper: ½ tsp
- Iodized salt: ¼ tsp (optional)
- Lean grated cheese: ½ cup (optional, for garnish)

Instructions:

1. Set the oven temperature to 375°F (190°C). Lightly grease a baking sheet with olive oil.
2. Slice the tops off the peppers and remove the seeds. Arrange the hollow peppers upright on the prepared baking sheet. Set aside.
3. Heat 1 tbsp olive oil in a large skillet over medium heat. Add the onion and garlic, saute for about 2 to 3 minutes until softened.
4. Add the ground turkey to the skillet. Cook until golden brown, breaking it up into smaller pieces with a spoon. This should take about 5 to 6 minutes.
5. Toss the zucchini, carrots, and spinach into the meat mixture. Cook for another 3 to 4 minutes until the vegetables begin to soften.
6. Season the mixture with cumin, smoked paprika, oregano, black pepper, and salt (if using).
7. Add the cooked quinoa or brown rice to the skillet. Add the low-sodium tomato sauce until well combined. Cook for 2 more minutes.
8. Add the filling evenly into each hollowed out pepper until full.
9. Cover the pan with foil and bake for 20 minutes. If you want a cheese topping, remove the foil after 20 minutes, sprinkle the grated low-fat cheese over each pepper, and bake uncovered for 5 more minutes or until the cheese is melted. Remove from the oven and let the stuffed peppers cool for a few minutes before serving.

Variants and substitutions:

For a vegetarian option, replace the ground turkey with ground chicken, lean ground beef, tofu, or cooked lentils.

Nutritional information (per serving): Calories: 250 kcal; Protein: 20g; Net Carbs: 14g; Fiber: 6g; Fat: 39g; Sugar: 7g (natural sugars from vegetables); Cholesterol: 75mg; Sodium: 300mg.

Turkey and Veggie Lettuce Wraps

Time: *10 min* ***Cook:*** *20 min* ***Servings****: 4*

Ingredients:

- Ground turkey (lean): 1 pound (93% lean recommended)
- Olive oil: 1 tbsp
- Onion: 1 small, finely chopped
- Garlic: 2 cloves, minced
- Carrot: 1 large, grated
- Red bell pepper: 1 small, diced
- Zucchini: 1 small, finely chopped
- Water chestnuts: ½ cup, chopped (optional for extra crunch)
- Soy sauce (low sodium): 3 tbsp
- Rice vinegar: 1 tbsp
- Hoisin sauce: 1 tbsp (optional, or substitute with sugar-free ketchup)
- Sriracha: 1 tbsp (optional for spice)
- Romaine lettuce leaves or butternut squash: 12 large leaves (for wraps)
- Green onions: 2 stalks, sliced (for garnish)
- Sesame seeds: 1 tsp (optional, for (to garnish)

Instructions:

1. Wash the lettuce leaves thoroughly and pat dry. Set aside on a plate to serve. Choose romaine or butter lettuce because they are large, sturdy, and hold the filling well.
2. In a large skillet, heat 1 tablespoon of olive oil over medium heat, add the chopped onion and garlic, and saute for 2-3 minutes until softened and fragrant.
3. Add the ground turkey to the skillet. Break it up with a spatula or wooden spoon, and cook for 5-7 minutes, until golden brown and cooked through.
4. Add the grated carrot, diced red bell pepper, zucchini, and water chestnuts (if using). Cook for another 3-4 minutes until the vegetables are slightly softened but still have a little crunch.
5. Season the mixture with soy sauce, rice vinegar, hoisin sauce (optional), and sriracha (optional for the spices). Stir well to combine all the flavors and cook for another 2 minutes to allow the turkey and vegetables to absorb the sauce.
6. Add the turkey and vegetable mixture to each lettuce leaf to form wraps. Garnish with sliced green onions and sesame seeds, if desired.
7. Serve the wraps immediately with additional garnishes on the side, such as extra sriracha or a sprinkle of fresh cilantro.

Variants and substitutions:

Replace the ground turkey with ground chicken, lean ground beef, or a plant-based alternative like tofu or tempeh, depending on your preference. Replace the ground turkey with crumbled tofu or tempeh and use vegan hoisin or soy sauce.

Nutritional information (per serving): Calories: 250 kcal; Protein: 35g; Net Carbs: 7g; Fiber: 5g; Fat: 30g; Sugar: 7g: Cholesterol: 80mg; Sodium: 500mg (varies by soy sauce).

Grilled Eggplant with Tomato and Feta

Time: *10 min* ***Cook:*** *25 min* ***Servings****: 4*

Ingredients:

- Eggplant: 2 medium (cut into ½-inch rounds)
- Olive oil: 3 tbsp
- Garlic powder: 1 tsp
- Dried oregano: 1 tsp
- Iodized salt: ½ tsp (or to taste)
- Cracked black pepper: ¼ tsp
- Cherry tomatoes: 2 cups (halved)
- Feta cheese: ½ cup (crumbled, use low-fat feta if preferred)
- Fresh basil: ¼ cup (coarsely chopped)
- Balsamic vinegar: 1 tbsp (optional, for extra flavor)

Instructions:

1. Slice the eggplant into ½-inch rounds and place on a large baking sheet or platter. Lightly sprinkle both sides of the eggplant slices with salt and let them sit for 10 to 15 minutes. This will draw out any excess moisture and reduce the bitterness. Then, use a paper towel to pat the eggplant dry.
2. Preheat the grill or grill pan to medium-high heat.
3. In a small bowl, combine the olive oil, garlic powder, oregano, salt, and pepper.
4. Brush both sides of the eggplant slices with the seasoned olive oil mixture.
5. Place the eggplant slices on the preheated grill or grill pan. Cook for 4 to 5 minutes on each side or until the eggplant is tender and has clear grill marks.
6. Remove the grilled eggplant from the grill and transfer to a serving platter.
7. In a bowl, combine the halved cherry tomatoes, a drizzle of olive oil, a pinch of salt, and optional balsamic vinegar. Toss gently to coat.
8. Arrange the grilled eggplant slices on a platter. Spread the tomato mixture over the top of the eggplant.
9. Sprinkle the plate with crumbled feta cheese and chopped fresh basil to garnish. Serve the grilled eggplant platter warm as a main course or side dish

Variants and substitutions:

Swap the feta cheese for vegan feta or a sprinkle of nutritional yeast for a dairy-free cheesy flavor. Try swapping out the basil for fresh mint, parsley, or oregano for a different flavor profile.

Nutritional information (per serving): Calories: 190 kcal; Protein: 10g; Net Carbs: 7g; Fiber: 10g; Fat: 40g; Sugar: 5g; Cholesterol: 0g; Sodium: 400mg.

Baked Cod with Lemon and Dill

Time: *10 min* ***Cook:*** *20 min* ***Servings****: 4*

Ingredients:

- Cod fillets: 4 (about 6 ounces each)
- Olive oil: 2 tbsp
- Fresh lemon juice: 2 tbsp
- Lemon zest: 1 tsp
- Fresh dill: 2 tbsp (minced)
- Garlic: 2 cloves (minced)
- Iodized salt ½ tsp (or to taste)
- Black pepper: ¼ teaspoon
- Paprika: ¼ tsp (optional, for color)
- Lemon slices: for garnish (optional)

Instructions:

1. Set the oven temperature to 200°C (400°F) and line a baking sheet with parchment paper or lightly grease it with a little olive oil.
2. Pat the cod fillets dry with paper towels to remove any excess moisture. This helps ensure a nice texture when cooked. Place them on the prepared baking sheet.
3. In a small bowl, whisk together the olive oil, fresh lemon juice, lemon zest, minced garlic, chopped dill, salt and pepper.
4. If you like, you can add a sprinkle of paprika for a little extra color and flavor.
5. Generously brush the lemon and dill mixture over each cod fillet, making sure to coat evenly.
6. Optionally, place a lemon wedge on top of each fillet for added flavor and presentation.
7. Place the baking sheet in the preheated oven and bake for 15-20 minutes. The cod is done when it flakes easily with a fork.
8. Garnish the baked cod with extra fresh dill and a squeeze of lemon juice, if desired.

Variants and substitutions:

If you don't have dill, you can substitute fresh parsley, basil, or cilantro for a different flavor profile. For a smoky flavor, you can also grill the cod instead of baking it. Simply place the fillets on a well-oiled grill and cook over medium heat for about 4-5 minutes per side.

Nutritional information (per serving): Calories: 220 kcal; Protein: 80g; Net Carbs: Negligible; Fiber: Negligible; Fat: 8g; Sugar: Negligible; Cholesterol: 0,75mg; Sodium: 300mg.

Roasted Vegetable Medley

Time: *15 min* ***Cook:*** *30 min* ***Servings****: 4*

Ingredients:

- Zucchini: 1 medium, sliced into rounds or half moons
- Red bell pepper: 1, chopped
- Yellow bell pepper: 1, chopped
- Red onion: 1 small, sliced into wedges
- Carrots: 2 medium, sliced diagonally or into rounds
- Broccoli florets: 2 cups (about 1 small head)
- Olive oil: 3 tbsp
- Garlic powder: 1 tsp
- Dried thyme: 1 tsp
- Dried rosemary: 1 tsp
- Iodized salt: ½ teaspoon (or to taste)
- Black pepper: ¼ tsp (or to taste)
- Fresh parsley: 2 tbsp, chopped (optional, for garnish)
- Lemon juice: 1 tbsp (optional, for a spicy finish)

Instructions:

1. Set the oven to 425°F (220°C) and line a large baking sheet with parchment paper or lightly grease it with olive oil.
2. Cut and slice all of the vegetables as directed in the ingredients. Try to get them to be uniform in size to ensure even cooking.
3. Broccoli florets can be kept slightly larger, while items like zucchini and bell peppers should be cut into smaller, bite-sized pieces.
4. In a large bowl, combine the vegetables (zucchini, bell peppers, onions, carrots, and broccoli).
5. Drizzle with olive oil and toss to coat evenly.
6. Add the seasonings: garlic powder, dried thyme, dried rosemary, salt, and pepper. Toss until the vegetables are well coated in the seasoning.
7. Spread the seasoned vegetables evenly on the prepared baking sheet. Make sure they are in a single layer for even cooking. Bake in the preheated oven for 25-30 minutes, stirring halfway through to ensure even cooking. The vegetables should be tender and slightly caramelized on the edges when cooked.
8. Once roasted, remove the vegetables from the oven.
9. Optionally, drizzle with fresh lemon juice for a bright, tangy flavor and garnish with chopped parsley. Serve warm as a side dish or with a lean protein like grilled chicken, fish, or tofu.

Variants and substitutions:

Instead of thyme and rosemary, you can use herbs like oregano, basil, or Italian seasoning for a different flavor profile. For those who like a little heat, sprinkle on some red pepper flakes or a pinch of cayenne before roasting.

Nutritional information (per serving): Calories: 140 kcal; Protein: 2g; Net Carbs: 10g; Fiber: 5g; Fat: 20g; Sugar: 8g; Cholestero:l 0g; Sodium: 200mg.

Turkey and Spinach Meatballs

Time: *15 min* ***Cook:*** *30 min* ***Servings****: 4*

Ingredients:

- Ground turkey (lean, 93% lean): 1 pound
- Fresh spinach: 2 cups (coarsely chopped or 1 cup frozen spinach, thawed and drained)
- Egg: 1 large (acts as a binder)
- Almond flour: ¼ cup (for low-carb diet; can substitute whole-wheat breadcrumbs if not on a low-carb diet)
- Garlic: 2 cloves, minced
- Onion: ¼ cup, finely chopped
- Dried oregano: 1 tsp
- Dried basil: 1 tsp
- Sea salt: ½ tsp (or to taste)
- Black pepper: ¼ tsp (or to taste)
- Olive oil: 2 tbsp (for cooking or to lightly grease the pan)

Instructions:

1. Set the oven temperature to 400°F (200°C) and lightly grease a baking sheet with olive oil or line it with parchment paper.
2. If using fresh spinach, lightly sauté it over medium heat for about 2 minutes until it wilts, then drain off any excess liquid and chop finely. If using frozen spinach, make sure it is completely thawed and drained to avoid excess moisture.
3. In a large bowl, combine the ground turkey, chopped spinach, egg, almond meal, garlic, onion, oregano, basil, salt, and pepper.
4. Use your hands or a spoon to gently mix everything together until well combined, being careful not to overmix (overmixing can make the meatballs tough).
5. Using your hands, shape the mixture into meatballs about 1 1/2 inches in diameter. You should have about 12-16 meatballs, depending on the size.
6. Place the meatballs on the prepared baking sheet, leaving some space between them. Bake in the preheated oven for 25-30 minutes, or until golden brown.
7. Once the meatballs are cooked, remove them from the oven and let them cool for a few minutes before serving.
8. Serve the turkey and spinach meatballs with a side of zucchini noodles, whole wheat pasta, or a salad for a complete meal.

Variants and substitutions:

To keep this dish gluten-free, use almond flour or coconut flour instead of breadcrumbs. For a more Mediterranean twist, add chopped sun-dried tomatoes and feta to the mix.

Nutritional information (per serving): Calories: 210 kcal; Protein: 45g; Net Carbs: 5g; Fiber: 5g; Fat: 30g; Sugar: Negligible.; Cholesterol: 100mg; Sodium: 380mg.

Butternut Squash Soup

Time: *15 min* ***Cook:*** *35 min* ***Servings****: 4*

Ingredients:

- Butternut squash: 1 large (about 2 pounds), peeled, seeded, and diced
- Olive oil: 1 tbsp
- Onion: 1 medium, diced
- Garlic: 2 cloves, minced
- Carrot: 1 medium, peeled and diced
- Celery: 1 stalk, diced
- Low-sodium chicken or vegetable broth: 4 cups
- Coconut milk (unsweetened, whole, or light): ½ cup (for creaminess)
- Ground cinnamon: ½ tsp
- Ground nutmeg: ¼ tsp
- Salt: ½ tsp (adjust to taste)
- Black pepper: ¼ teaspoon
- Fresh thyme (optional): 1 tsp, minced (or ½ teaspoon dried)
- Pumpkin seeds (optional): for garnish

Instructions:

1. Peel and dice the butternut squash. The cubes should be about 1 inch in size for even cooking.
2. In a large stockpot or Dutch oven, heat 1 tablespoon of the olive oil over medium heat, add the onion, garlic, carrot, and celery, and cook, stirring occasionally, until the vegetables are softened and fragrant, about 5 minutes.
3. Add the diced butternut squash to the pot, stir to combine with the sautéed vegetables, and cook for another 3 to 4 minutes.
4. Pour in 4 cups of low-sodium vegetable or chicken broth, making sure the squash is completely submerged.
5. Add the ground cinnamon, ground nutmeg, salt, black pepper, and thyme (if using). Bring the mixture to a boil, then reduce the heat to low, cover the pot, and simmer for 20 minutes, or until the butternut squash is very tender.
6. Once the squash is tender, remove the pot from the heat.
7. Using an immersion blender, blend the soup until smooth and creamy. (If using a stand blender, blend the soup in batches, making sure not to overfill the blender to avoid spillage.) Stir in the coconut milk for extra creaminess and adjust seasoning if necessary.
8. Ladle the soup into bowls and garnish with pumpkin seeds or a drizzle of olive oil for added texture and flavor.
9. Serve warm.

Variants and substitutions:

Instead of coconut milk, you can use unsweetened almond milk or Greek yogurt (added after blending the soup) to reduce the fat content while keeping it creamy.

Nutritional information (per serving): Calories: 160 kcal; Protein: 5g; Net Carbs: 20g; Fiber: 10g; Fat: 10g; Sugar: 4g; Cholesterol 0g; Sodium 250mg.

Chickpea and Vegetable Curry

Time: *10 min* ***Cook:*** *30 min* ***Servings****: 4*

Ingredients:

- Olive oil: 1 tbsp
- Onion: 1 medium, diced
- Garlic: 3 cloves, minced
- Ginger: 1 tbsp, freshly grated
- Carrots: 2 medium, diced
- Red bell pepper: 1, diced
- Zucchini: 1 medium, diced
- Chickpeas: 2 cans (15 oz each), drained and rinsed
- Diced tomatoes: 1 can (15 oz)
- Coconut milk (unsweetened): 1 can (13.5 oz, light or whole)
- Curry powder: 2 tbsp
- Cumin powder: 1 tsp
- Turmeric powder: ½ tsp
- Coriander powder: ½ tsp
- Paprika or cayenne pepper (optional, for heat): ¼ tsp
- Spinach: 2 cups fresh or 1 cup frozen
- Low-sodium vegetable broth: ½ cup (optional, to thin the curry)
- Low-sodium salt: ½ tsp (adjust to taste)
- Black pepper: ¼ tsp
- Fresh cilantro (optional, to garnish)
- Lime wedges (optional, to serve)

Instructions:

1. Heat 1 tbsp of the olive oil in a large pot or Dutch oven over medium heat, adding the diced onion and cooking until translucent, about 5 minutes. Add the minced garlic and grated ginger and cook for another minute.
2. Add the diced carrots, red bell pepper and zucchini to the pot. Cook for about 3 to 4 minutes, stirring occasionally, until the vegetables begin to soften.
3. Add the curry powder, ground cumin, ground turmeric, ground coriander and paprika or cayenne (if using for heat). Toast the spices for 1 minute, allowing the flavors to bloom.
4. Add the drained and rinsed chickpeas and diced tomatoes to the pot, stirring to combine with the spiced vegetables.
5. Pour in the coconut milk and bring the mixture to a boil. If the curry seems too thick, add 1/2 cup vegetable stock to thin it out if necessary.
6. Reduce the heat and let the curry simmer uncovered for 15 minutes, stirring occasionally. This allows the flavors to meld and the vegetables to fully soften.
7. Stir in the fresh spinach (or frozen spinach, if using) and cook for another 2-3 minutes, until the spinach wilts in the curry. Taste and season with salt and black pepper, if necessary.
8. Remove the curry from the heat and let it cool for a few minutes before serving. Garnish with fresh cilantro and serve with lime wedges on the side for a tangy finish.

Variants and substitutions:

If you prefer a richer curry, use full-fat coconut milk instead of the light version.

Nutritional information (per serving): Calories: 260 kcal; Protein: 9g; Net Carbs: 32g; Fiber: 12g; Fat: 40g; Sugar: 10g; Cholesterol 0g; Sodium 400mg.

Grilled Shrimp with Zucchini Noodles

Time: *15 min* ***Cook:*** *15 min* ***Servings****: 4*

Ingredients:

For the grilled shrimp:

- Shrimp (large, shelled and gutted): 1 ½ pounds
- Olive oil: 1 tbsp
- Garlic (minced): 2 cloves
- Lemon juice: 2 tbsp (freshly squeezed)
- Lemon zest: 1 tsp
- Paprika: 1 tsp
- Cayenne pepper (optional, for heat): ¼ tsp
- Salt: ½ tsp
- Black pepper: ¼ tsp
- Fresh parsley: 2 tbsp (minced, for garnish)

For the zucchini noodles (Zoodles):

- Zucchini: 4 medium (spiralized into spaghetti)
- Olive oil: 1 tbsp
- Garlic (minced): 2 cloves
- Cherries: 1 cup, halved
- Parmesan cheese (optional): ¼ cup, freshly grated
- Fresh basil: 2 tbsp(chopped)
- Red chili flakes: ¼ teaspoon (optional)
- Salt and pepper: To taste

Instructions:

1. In a large bowl, combine 1 tbsp oil, garlic, lemon juice, lemon zest, bell pepper, cayenne pepper (if using), salt, and black pepper. Add shrimp and toss to coat evenly. Refrigerate covered for 15 min.
2. Using a spiralizer, make noodles from the zucchini and set aside. No spiralizer? You can use a julienne peeler or slice the zucchini thinly with a knife.
3. Heat 1 tbsp olive oil in a large skillet over medium heat. Add the minced garlic and sauté for about 1 minute until fragrant.
4. Add the zucchini noodles to the skillet and cook for 2-3 minutes, stirring occasionally, until the noodles are slightly softened but still crispy.
5. Add the halved cherry tomatoes, red pepper flakes (optional), and salt and pepper to taste. Cook for another minute. Remove from heat and stir in the chopped basil. If using, sprinkle with parmesan cheese before serving.
6. Preheat a grill or broiler pan to medium-high heat. Thread the marinated shrimp onto skewers (wooden skewers soaked in water for 30 minutes to prevent burning). Grill shrimp 2-3 minutes per side or until pink and opaque. Do not overcook shrimp, as they may become rubbery.
7. Serve and, if desired, add a squeeze of lemon.

Variants and substitutions:

Instead of zucchini spaghetti, you can use squash spaghetti, carrot spaghetti, or a mix of vegetable spaghetti for a bit of variety.

Nutritional information (per serving): Calories: 240 kcal; Protein: 27g; Net Carbs: 7g; Fiber: 3g; Fat: 20g; Sugar: 5g; Cholesterol 170mg; Sodium 500mg.

Baked Chicken with Brussels Sprouts

Time: *10 min* ***Cook:*** *35 min* ***Servings****: 4*

Ingredients:

- Chicken breasts (boneless, skinless): 4 (about 1 pound total)
- Brussels sprouts (halved): 1 pound
- Olive oil: 3 tbsp
- Garlic (minced): 3 cloves
- Lemon zest: 1 tsp
- Lemon juice: 2 tbsp
- Dijon mustard: 1 tbsp
- Dried thyme: 1 tsp
- Paprika: 1 tsp
- Salt: 1 tsp
- Black pepper: ½ tsp
- Fresh parsley: 2 tbsp (chopped, for garnish)
- Parmesan cheese (optional): ¼ cup (grated)

Instructions:

1. Set the oven temperature to 400°F (200°C). Line a large baking sheet or cookie sheet with parchment paper or lightly grease it with olive oil.
2. In a small bowl, combine 1 tablespoon olive oil, minced garlic, lemon zest, lemon juice, Dijon mustard, dried thyme, paprika, salt, and black pepper.
3. Arrange the chicken breasts on the prepared baking sheet and brush or rub the marinade over the chicken, making sure each piece is well coated. Set aside to absorb the flavors while.
4. In a large bowl, toss the halved Brussels sprouts with 2 tablespoons olive oil, a pinch of salt, and pepper. Make sure they are evenly coated.
5. Arrange the Brussels sprouts around the chicken breasts on the baking sheet. Spread them out in a single layer for even cooking.
6. Place the pan in the oven and roast for 25-30 minutes or until the chicken and Brussels sprouts are tender with crispy, caramelized edges. If the Brussels sprouts cook faster than the chicken, you can remove them first and let the chicken continue to cook until done.
7. For a more golden finish, turn on the broiler for the last 2-3 minutes of cooking to crisp up the chicken skin and Brussels sprouts.
8. Once cooked, remove the pan from the oven. Let the chicken rest for 5 minutes before slicing. Garnish with fresh parsley and sprinkle grated Parmesan cheese over the Brussels sprouts, if using.
9. Serve warm with lemon wedges on the side for an extra burst of flavor.

Variants and substitutions:

If Brussels sprouts aren't your favorite, you can substitute other non-starchy vegetables like broccoli, cauliflower, or green beans. Swap the paprika and thyme for Italian seasoning, rosemary, or cumin for a different flavor profile.

Nutritional information (per serving): Calories: 280 kcal; Protein: 35g; Net Carbs: 5g; Fiber: 5g; Fat: 18g; Sugar: 2g; Cholesterol 90mg; Sodium 590mg.

Tofu and Broccoli Stir-Fry

Time: *10 min* ***Cook:*** *35 min* ***Servings****: 4*

Ingredients:

- Extra-firm tofu: 14 oz (1 block), drained and pressed
- Broccoli florets: 3 cups
- Olive oil: 3 tbsp (divided)
- Low-sodium soy sauce: 3 tbsp
- Rice vinegar: 1 tbsp
- Fresh ginger: 1 tbsp, minced
- Garlic: 3 cloves, minced
- Sesame oil: 1 tsp (optional for flavor)
- Cornstarch: 1 tbsp (to thicken sauce)
- Water: ¼ cup (for sauce)
- Red bell pepper: 1, thinly sliced (optional for color and sweetness)
- Green onions: 2, thinly sliced for garnish
- Sesame seeds: 1 tbsp (optional for garnish)

Instructions:

1. Wrap the tofu in paper towels or a clean dish towel and place something heavy (like a pan or books) on top to squeeze out the excess moisture. Let it sit for 10 to 15 minutes. This helps the tofu crisp up as it cooks. Once pressed, cut the tofu into 1-inch cubes.
2. In a small bowl, whisk together the low-sodium soy sauce, rice vinegar, minced ginger, minced garlic, and sesame oil (if using). Set aside.
3. In another bowl, dissolve the cornstarch in ¼ cup water to create a paste. This will thicken the stir-fry sauce.
4. Heat 2 tablespoons olive oil in a large nonstick skillet or wok over medium-high heat. Once hot, add the tofu cubes in a single layer and cook until golden brown and crispy on all sides, about 4-5 minutes per side. Use tongs or a spatula to carefully flip the tofu. Once the tofu is crispy, remove it from the pan and set aside.
5. In the same pan, heat the remaining tablespoon of olive oil. Add the broccoli florets and sliced red bell pepper (if using). Sauté for about 4-5 minutes until the vegetables are crispy and tender but still bright in color.
6. Add the crispy tofu back to the pan with the vegetables. Pour in the prepared stir-fry sauce and cornstarch batter. Gently toss everything together and cook for another 2-3 minutes, or until the sauce thickens and evenly coats the tofu and vegetables.
7. Remove from the heat and serve the stir-fry hot. Garnish with sliced scallions and sesame seeds, if desired.

Variants and substitutions:

No soy? Replace tofu with chickpeas or seitan (wheat gluten). No tofu? Use chicken, shrimp or beef.

Nutritional information (per serving): Calories: 230 kcal; Protein: 30g; Fiber: 6g; Fat: 25g; Sugar: 3g; Net Carbs: 14g; Cholesterol 0g; Sodium 450mg.

Eggplant and Tomato Baked

Time: *15 min* ***Cook:*** *30 min* ***Servings****: 4*

Ingredients:

- Eggplant: 2 medium (about 1 pound)
- Fresh tomatoes: 4 medium (or 1 can diced tomatoes, 14.5 ounces)
- Olive oil: 3 tbsp
- Garlic: 3 cloves, minced
- Onion: 1 medium, minced
- Fresh basil: ½ cup, minced (or 1 tbsp dried basil)
- Italian seasoning: 1 tsp
- Salt: ½ tsp (or to taste)
- Black pepper: ¼ tsp
- Parmesan cheese: ½ cup, grated (optional for garnish)
- Mozzarella cheese: 1 cup, grated (optional for garnish)
- Red chili flakes: ¼ tsp (optional for spiciness)

Instructions:

1. Set the oven temperature to 375°F (190°C).
2. Slice the eggplant into ½-inch thick slices. Sprinkle both sides with salt and let sit for about 10 minutes to remove excess moisture. This helps reduce the bitterness.
3. While the eggplant is resting, heat 2 tbsp of olive oil in a large skillet over medium heat. Add onion and sauté for about 3-4 minutes until softened, then add the minced garlic and saute for another minute until fragrant.
4. Add the tomatoes (fresh or canned) to the skillet with the onions and garlic. Add the Italian seasoning, black pepper, and red pepper flakes (if using). Simmer for about 5-7 minutes, until the tomatoes have softened and released their juices.
5. After 10 minutes, rinse the eggplant slices under cold water to remove excess salt and pat dry with a paper towel.
6. In a separate skillet, heat olive oil over medium heat. Add the eggplant slices in a single layer and cook until golden brown, about 3 to 4 minutes per side. Remove and set aside.
7. In a baking dish, spread a thin layer of tomato mixture on the bottom, then arrange eggplant slices on top. Add more tomato mixture on top, followed by half of the fresh basil. Repeat layers with remaining eggplant, tomato mixture, and basil. If using, sprinkle grated parmesan and mozzarella evenly on top.
8. Cover the dish with aluminum foil and bake in the oven for 20 minutes. Then remove the foil and bake for another 10 minutes, or until the cheese is bubbly and lightly golden.
9. Let the cake cool for a few minutes before cutting. Serve warm, garnished with extra fresh basil if desired.

Variants and substitutions:

To obtain a dish with a low fat and calorie content, use low-fat cheeses or omit them altogether.

Nutritional information (per serving): Calories: 190 kcal; Protein: 15g; Fiber: 12g; Fat: 40g; Sugar: 4g; Net Carbs: 12g; Cholesterol 15mg; Sodium 320mg.

Stir-Fried Tofu with Mixed Vegetables

Time: *10 min* ***Cook:*** *20 min* ***Servings****: 4*

Ingredients:

- Firm or extra-firm tofu: 14 oz (1 block), drained and cubed
- Broccoli florets: 2 cups
- Peppers: 1 large, thinly sliced (any color)
- Carrots: 2 medium, julienned or thinly sliced
- Zucchini: 1 medium, thinly sliced
- Sweet peas or sugar snap peas: 1 cup (optional)
- Garlic: 3 cloves, minced
- Ginger: 1 tbsp, freshly grated
- Green onions: 2, thinly sliced for garnish (optional)
- Low-sodium soy sauce or tamari: 3 tbsp (for gluten-free, use tamari)
- Rice vinegar: 1 tbsp
- Sesame oil: 1 tbsp
- Vegetable broth: ¼ cup (or water)
- Cornstarch: 1 tsp (for thicken, optional)
- Red chili flakes: ¼ tsp (optional for heat)
- Sesame seeds: 1 tbsp (optional for garnish)
- Olive oil or avocado oil: 2 tbsp (divided use)

Instructions:

1. Drain the tofu and press it for 10-15 minutes to remove excess moisture. After pressing, cut the tofu into 1-inch cubes.
2. Wash and chop the vegetables. Keep them uniform in size for even cooking. Broccoli florets, bell peppers, carrots, and zucchini work well, but feel free to use other vegetables like sugar snap peas or mushrooms.
3. Heat 1 tbsp of olive oil in a large skillet or wok over medium-high heat. Once hot, add the cubed tofu in a single layer. Cook for about 3-4 minutes per side until the tofu is golden. Remove and set aside.
4. In the same skillet, add the remaining tbsp of oil. Add the garlic and ginger and sauté for about 30 seconds, until fragrant.
5. Add the broccoli, carrots, and zucchini to the skillet and sauté for 5 to 7 minutes, until the vegetables are tender but still crisp. Add the bell peppers and snap peas and cook for another 2 to 3 minutes.
6. In a small bowl, whisk the soy sauce, rice vinegar, sesame oil, broth, and cornstarch (if using). Add red chili flakes, if desired.
7. Return the cooked tofu to the skillet with the vegetables. Pour the sauce over the tofu and vegetables. Cook for another 2 or 3 minutes, allowing the sauce to thicken slightly.
8. Remove from the heat and garnish with sliced green onions and sesame seeds (optional). Serve warm, on its own or with brown rice or cauliflower rice for a low-carb option.

Variants and substitutions:

If you prefer animal protein, replace the tofu with tempeh, seitan, or even chicken or shrimp. To make this dish gluten-free, be sure to use tamari or gluten-free soy sauce.

Nutritional information (per serving): Calories: 230 kcal; Protein: 20g; Fiber: 4g; Fat: 25g; Sugar: 5g; Net Carbs: 11g; Cholesterol 0g; Sodium 540mg.

Chicken Fajitas with Grilled Peppers and Onions

Time: *15 min* ***Cook:*** *25 min* ***Servings****: 4*

Ingredients:

- Chicken breast: 1 pound, boneless and skinless, sliced
- Peppers: 3 medium (mix of colors: red, yellow, green), thinly sliced
- Onion: 1 large, thinly sliced
- Olive oil: 2 tbsp, divided
- Chili powder: 1 tsp
- Cumin: 1 tsp
- Paprika: 1 tsp
- Garlic powder: ½ tsp
- Onion powder: ½ tsp
- Dried oregano: ½ tsp
- Cracked black pepper: ¼ tsp
- Salt: ¼ tsp (optional or reduce for low sodium)
- Red chili flakes: ¼ tsp (optional, for spiciness)
- Low-carb tortillas: 4 medium (or use lettuce wraps for a low-carb option)
- Fresh cilantro: ¼ cup, chopped (optional)
- Lime wedges: 2, for serving
- Avocado: 1 large, sliced
- Salsa: ½ cup (store-bought or homemade, no added sugar)
- Greek yogurt: ¼ cup (healthy alternative to sour cream)

Instructions:

1. Cut the chicken breasts into thin strips and place in a bowl.
2. In another bowl, combine the chili powder, cumin, paprika, garlic powder, onion powder, oregano, black pepper, and salt. Mix well.
3. Coat the chicken strips with 1 tablespoon of the olive oil and drizzle half of the seasoning mix over the chicken. Toss to coat evenly.
4. Thinly slice the bell peppers and onion.
5. Heat the remaining tablespoon of olive oil in a large skillet over medium heat, and add the sliced onions and bell peppers. Drizzle the remaining seasoning mix over the vegetables and sauté for 5 to 7 minutes until soft but still slightly crisp. Remove the vegetables from the skillet and set aside.
6. To the same skillet, add the seasoned chicken strips. Cook for 6 to 8 minutes, stirring occasionally, until the chicken is golden and cooked through. Add the cooked peppers and onions with the chicken and stir for another 2 minutes to combine the flavors.
7. While the chicken and vegetables are finishing cooking, heat the tortillas in a dry skillet or directly over a flame for 30 seconds on each side, just to warm them through.
8. Serve the chicken and vegetable mixture on the warmed tortillas (or lettuce wraps)
9. Garnish with fresh cilantro, sliced avocado, Greek yogurt, and a squeeze of lime. Add a spoonful of salsa to each fajita for extra flavor.

Variants and substitutions:

For a protein alternative, replace the chicken with lean beef strips, shrimp, or tofu. Instead of Greek yogurt, use lactose-free yogurt or avoid it altogether.

Nutritional information (per serving): Calories: 320 kcal; Protein: 50g; Net Carbs: 14g; Fiber: 6g; Sugars: 6g; Fat: 30g; Cholesterol 65mg; Sodium 200mg.

Grilled Vegetable Salad with Feta

Time: *15 min* ***Cook:*** *25 min* ***Servings****: 4*

Ingredients:

- Zucchini: 2 medium, sliced into rounds
- Peppers: 2 medium (choose a variety of colors), sliced into thick strips
- Red onion: 1 large, sliced into thick rounds
- Asparagus: 1 bunch, tough ends trimmed
- Cherry tomatoes: 1 pint (serve raw or lightly grilled)
- Olive oil: 5 tbsp
- Garlic powder: ½ tsp
- Dried oregano: ½ tsp
- Low-sodium salt: ½ tsp (optional)
- Cracked black pepper: ¼ tsp
- Feta cheese: ½ cup, crumbled
- Lemon juice: 2 tbsp
- Dijon mustard: 1 tsp
- Red wine vinegar: 1 tbsp
- Garlic: 1 clove, minced
- Fresh parsley: 2 tbsp, minced (optional)

Instructions:

1. Preheat grill to medium-high heat (or use a grill pan if you're indoors).
2. In a large bowl, toss the zucchini, bell peppers, red onion, and asparagus with 3 tablespoons of the olive oil, garlic powder, dried oregano, salt, and pepper.
3. Grill the zucchini and bell peppers for 3 to 4 minutes per side until lightly charred and tender.
4. Grill the onion slices for about 4 to 5 minutes per side until softened and caramelized.
5. Grill the asparagus for about 3 to 5 minutes, turning occasionally, until just tender.
6. While the vegetables are grilling, whisk together the olive oil, lemon juice, Dijon mustard, red wine vinegar, and minced garlic in a small bowl. Season the dressing with salt and pepper to taste, and add the fresh parsley for extra flavor.
7. Once the vegetables are grilled, arrange them on a large serving platter. Evenly distribute the grilled vegetables and cherry tomatoes on the platter.
8. Drizzle the prepared lemon vinaigrette over the vegetables, making sure to coat them evenly.
9. Garnish the grilled vegetable salad with the crumbled feta cheese. Garnish with extra parsley or a sprinkle of oregano, if desired.

Variants and substitutions:

Omit the feta or replace with plant-based feta or tofu for a dairy-free version. Add grilled chicken, shrimp, or tofu for a heartier main dish.

Nutritional information (per serving): Calories: 210 kcal; Protein: 6g; Fiber: 4g; Fat: 25g; Sugar: 6g; Net Carbs: 16g; Cholesterol 10mg; Sodium 380mg.

Baked Lemon Garlic Chicken

Time: *10 min* ***Cook:*** *30 min* ***Servings***: *4*

Ingredients:

- Boneless, skinless chicken breasts: 4 (about 1.5 pounds total)
- Olive oil: 2 tbsp
- Garlic: 4 cloves, minced
- Lemon juice: ¼ cup (about 1 large lemon)
- Lemon zest: 1 tsp (optional)
- Dried oregano: 1 tsp
- Dried thyme: ½ tsp
- Paprika: ½ tsp (for color and flavor)
- Low-sodium salt: ½ tsp (optional)
- Cracked black pepper: ¼ tsp
- Fresh parsley: 2 tbsp, chopped (optional, for garnish)

Instructions:

1. Set the oven temperature to 400°F (200°C).
2. Pat the chicken breasts dry with paper towels to remove excess moisture, and arrange them on a baking sheet in a single layer.
3. In a small bowl, whisk together the olive oil, minced garlic, lemon juice, lemon zest, oregano, thyme, paprika, salt, and pepper.
4. Pour the lemon-garlic marinade evenly over the chicken breasts, making sure they are well coated.
5. Marinate the chicken for 10 to 15 minutes for extra flavor (but not necessary if you're short on time).
6. Place the baking sheet in the oven and bake for 25 to 30 minutes. Halfway through cooking, baste the chicken with the cooking juices to keep it moist.
7. Remove the chicken from the oven and let it rest for 5 minutes to allow the juices to redistribute.
8. Garnish with fresh parsley and serve the Baked Lemon Garlic Chicken with your favorite steamed vegetables, quinoa, or brown rice.

Variants and substitutions:

Swap out the oregano and thyme for rosemary or basil for a different herb profile. Add slice zucchini, cherry tomatoes, or carrots to the pan with the chicken for a one-pan meal.

Nutritional information (per serving): Calories: 280 kcal; Protein: 32g; Fiber: 2g; Fat: 30g; Sugar: 6g; Net Carbs: 3g; Cholesterol 90mg; Sodium 300mg.

Herb-Roasted Chicken Thighs

Time: *10 min* ***Cook:*** *35 min* ***Servings****: 4*

Ingredients:

- Bone-in, skin-on chicken thighs: 4 (about 1.5 pounds total)
- Olive oil: 2 tbsp
- Fresh rosemary: 1 tbsp, finely chopped
- Fresh thyme: 1 tbsp, finely chopped
- Garlic: 3 cloves, minced
- Lemon juice: 2 tbsp (from 1 lemon)
- Paprika: 1 tsp
- Low-sodium salt: ½ tsp
- Cracked black pepper: ¼ tsp
- Lemon zest: 1 tsp (optional, for extra flavor)
- Fresh parsley: 1 tbsp, chopped (for garnish)

Instructions:

1. Set the oven temperature to 400°F (200°C).
2. Pat the chicken thighs dry with paper towels to remove excess moisture. This helps the skin crisp up.
3. Place the chicken thighs on a baking sheet or rimmed baking sheet.
4. In a small bowl, whisk together the olive oil, rosemary, thyme, garlic, lemon juice, paprika, salt, and pepper. Optionally, add lemon zest for an extra burst of flavor.
5. Rub the herb marinade evenly over the chicken thighs, making sure to get it under the skin for maximum flavor.
6. Place the chicken in the preheated oven and roast for 30 to 35 minutes or until the skin is golden brown and crispy. Halfway through cooking, baste the chicken with any juices that collect in the pan to keep it moist.
7. Remove the chicken from the oven and let it rest for 5 minutes before serving. This allows the juices to redistribute and the chicken to stay moist.
8. Garnish the chicken with chopped parsley and serve with your favorite sides, such as roasted vegetables or cauliflower rice for a low-carb option.

Variants and substitutions:

Add a pinch of red pepper flakes or cayenne pepper to the marinade for a spicy kick. Add slices of zucchini, mushrooms, or carrots to the pan for a one-pan meal.

Nutritional information (per serving): Calories: 300 kcal; Protein: 25g; Fiber: Negligible; Fat: 20g; Sugar: 0g; Net Carbs: 0g; Cholesterol 115mg; Sodium 320mg.

Balsamic Glazed salmon

Time: *10 min* ***Cook:*** *25 min* ***Servings****: 4*

Ingredients:

- Salmon fillets: 4 (about 5-6 ounces each)
- Olive oil: 1 tbsp
- Balsamic vinegar: ⅓ cup
- Honey: 1 tbsp (optional, for sweetness; use a sugar substitute like stevia for a lower-sugar version)
- Garlic: 3 cloves, minced
- Dijon mustard: 1 tsp
- Fresh rosemary: 1 tsp, minced (or ½ tsp dried rosemary)
- Low-sodium salt: ½ tsp
- Black pepper: ¼ tsp
- Lemon juice: 1 tbsp (optional, for extra zing)

Instructions:

1. Set the oven temperature to 400°F (200°C).
2. In a small saucepan, combine the balsamic vinegar, honey (or sugar substitute), minced garlic, Dijon mustard, and rosemary.
3. Bring to a boil over medium heat, stirring occasionally. Cook until the glaze thickens and is reduced by half, about 5 to 6 minutes. Remove from heat and set aside.
4. While the glaze is reducing, prepare the salmon fillets. Pat them dry with a paper towel to remove excess moisture, and season both sides with salt and black pepper. Lightly brush each fillet with olive oil to help crisp the skin as it cooks.
5. Place the seasoned salmon fillets on a parchment-lined baking sheet, skin-side down.
6. Bake in the preheated oven for 12 to 15 minutes, depending on the thickness of the fillets.
7. During the last 5 minutes of cooking, brush the top of each fillet with the balsamic glaze. Return the salmon to the oven for the remaining cooking time, allowing the glaze to caramelize slightly on the fish.
8. Remove the salmon from the oven and pour the remaining balsamic glaze over the fillets before serving. Optionally, drizzle with fresh lemon juice for a brighter finish.

Variants and substitutions:

Substitute thyme or basil for the rosemary for a different, herbal flavor. If you prefer to grill, cook the salmon on a grill over medium heat for about 4-5 minutes per side, brushing with the glaze as it cooks.

Nutritional information (per serving): Calories: 310 kcal; Protein: 30g; Fiber: Negligible; Fat: 18g; Sugar: 4g; Net Carbs: 5g; Cholesterol 75mg; Sodium 320mg.

Vegetable and Bean Soup

Time: *10 min* ***Cook:*** *35 min* ***Servings****: 4*

Ingredients:

- Olive oil: 2 tbsp
- Onion: 1 medium, chopped
- Garlic: 3 cloves, minced
- Carrots: 2 medium, diced
- Celery: 2 stalks, diced
- Zucchini: 1 medium, chopped
- Green beans: 1 cup, rinsed and chopped
- Canned tomatoes, diced: 1 can (14.5 ounces), no salt added
- Canned carnelian beans (or any white bean): 1 can (15 ounces), drained and rinsed
- Low-sodium vegetable broth: 4 cups
- Water: 1 cup
- Fresh spinach: 2 cups, compressed (or use kale)
- Dried thyme: 1 tsp
- Dried oregano: 1 tsp
- Bay leaf: 1
- Salt: ½ tsp (adjust to taste)
- Black pepper: ¼ tsp (or to taste)
- Juice lemon: 1 tbsp (optional, for extra brightness)

Instructions:

1. Chop all the vegetables (onion, carrots, celery, zucchini, green beans) and set aside.
2. In a large pot or Dutch oven, heat the olive oil over medium heat. Add the onion and cook until softened, about 3-4 minutes, then add the garlic and sauté for another 30 minutes.
3. Toss together the carrots, celery, zucchini, and green beans. Cook for about 5 minutes, stirring occasionally, until the vegetables begin to soften.
4. Add the canned diced tomatoes (with juice), cannellini beans, vegetable broth, and water to the pot.
5. Add the thyme, oregano, bay leaves, salt, and black pepper.
6. Bring the soup to a boil, then reduce the heat to a simmer. Cover and cook for 20-25 minutes, until the vegetables are tender.
7. In the last 5 minutes of cooking, add the fresh spinach (or kale). Let it wilt in the soup.
8. Taste the soup and adjust the seasoning if necessary (add more salt, pepper or a splash of lemon juice for a more lively touch).
9. Remove the bay leaf before serving.

Variants and substitutions:

Use other non-starchy vegetables like peppers, broccoli, or cauliflower, depending on what you have on hand. Instead of spinach, you can use kale, Swiss chard, or even collard greens.

Nutritional information (per serving): Calories: 210 kcal; Protein: 10g; Fiber: 10g; Fat: 15g; Sugar: 8g; Net Carbs: 30g; Cholesterol 0g; Sodium 450mg.

Spicy Lentil Soup

Time: *10 min* ***Cook:*** *35 min* ***Servings****: 4*

Ingredients:

- Olive oil: 1 tbsp
- Onion: 1 medium, finely chopped
- Garlic: 4 cloves, minced
- Carrot: 2 medium, diced
- Celery: 2 stalks, diced
- Ground cumin: 2 tsp
- Ground coriander: 1 tsp
- Ground turmeric: 1 tsp
- Ground paprika (smoked or sweet): 1 tsp
- Cayenne pepper (optional): ¼ tsp
- Green or brown lentils: 1 cup, rinsed and drained
- Low-sodium vegetable broth: 6 cups
- Canned diced tomatoes: 1 can (14.5 ounces), no salt added
- Bay leaf: 1
- Fresh spinach or kale: 2 cups, chopped
- Fresh lemon juice: 2 tbsp
- Salt: ½ tsp (or to taste)
- Black pepper: ¼ tsp (or to pleasure)
- Fresh cilantro or parsley: ¼ cup, chopped (optional, for garnish)

Instructions:

1. Heat 1 tablespoon olive oil in a large pot over medium heat.
2. Add onion, carrot, and celery. Cook for 5 to 7 minutes, stirring occasionally, until vegetables are softened.
3. Add garlic and cook for another 30 seconds until fragrant.
4. Add ground cumin, coriander, turmeric, paprika, and cayenne pepper (if using). Cook for another 1 to 2 minutes to toast the spices and release their flavors.
5. Add lentils, vegetable broth, diced tomatoes, and bay leaf. Stir to combine and bring mixture to a boil.
6. Once boiling, reduce heat to low and cover pot. Cook for 25 to 30 minutes or until lentils are tender but not mushy. Stir occasionally.
7. In the last 5 minutes of cooking, add spinach or kale until wilted. Remove bay leaf. Add lemon juice and season the soup with salt and pepper to taste.
8. Ladle the soup into bowls and garnish with fresh cilantro or parsley, if desired.

Variants and substitutions:

If you don't have spinach or kale, try using Swiss chard or collard greens. Feel free to add other greens like zucchini, sweet potatoes, or butternut squash for more texture and flavor.

Nutritional information (per serving): Calories: 240 kcal; Protein: 20g; Fiber: 15g; Fat: 15g; Sugar: 6g; Net Carbs: 35g.; Cholesterol 0g; Sodium 430mg.

Baked Tilapia with Lemon and Herbs

Time: *10 min* ***Cook:*** *25 min* ***Servings****: 4*

Ingredients:

- Tilapia fillets: 4 (about 4-6 ounces each)
- Olive oil: 2 tbsp
- Lemon: 1, thinly sliced
- Fresh garlic: 3 cloves, minced
- Fresh parsley: ¼ cup, minced (or use cilantro or dill)
- Fresh thyme: 1 tbsp (or 1 tsp dried thyme)
- Fresh dill: 1 tbsp, minced (optional for extra flavor)
- Salt: ½ tsp (or to taste)
- Black pepper: ¼ tsp (or to taste)
- Paprika: 1 tsp (for color and flavor)
- Lemon zest: 1 tsp (optional, for extra lemony flavor)

Instructions:

1. Set the oven temperature to 400°F (200°C) and line a baking sheet with parchment paper or lightly grease with olive oil.
2. Rinse the tilapia fillets under cold water and pat dry with paper towels. Season both sides of the fillets with salt, pepper, and paprika.
3. In a small bowl, whisk together the olive oil, minced garlic, fresh parsley, thyme, and dill (if using). Add the lemon juice and toss well.
4. Place the seasoned tilapia fillets on the prepared baking sheet.
5. Drizzle or brush the herb and garlic mixture evenly over the fillets, making sure each fillet is well coated.
6. Place lemon slices on each fillet for a hint of fresh, tangy flavor. Optionally, sprinkle with lemon zest for extra zing.
7. Place the pan in the preheated oven and bake for 15-20 minutes or until the fish is opaque and flakes easily with a fork.
8. If desired, cook the fillets for an additional 2-3 minutes at the end of cooking to achieve a slightly crispy, golden finish.
9. Remove the cooked tilapia from the oven and serve immediately. Garnish with extra fresh herbs and a squeeze of fresh lemon juice, if desired.

Variants and substitutions:

Try cilantro, basil, or oregano in place of parsley and thyme for a different flavor profile. For extra heat, sprinkle the fillets with red pepper flakes or cayenne pepper before baking.

Nutritional information (per serving): Calories: 220kcal; Protein: 30g; Fiber: Negligible; Fat: 1g; Sugar: Negligible; Net Carbs: 0g. Cholesterol 70mg; Sodium 350mg.

Chicken and Vegetable Stir-Fry

Time: *10 min* ***Cook:*** *20 min* ***Servings****: 4*

Ingredients:

- Boneless chicken: 1 pound skinless breast, thinly sliced
- Olive oil: 2 tbps (or avocado oil)
- Large bell pepper (any color): 1, thinly sliced
- Medium zucchini: 1, sliced into half moons
- Broccoli florets: 1 cup
- Medium carrot: 1, thinly sliced
- Red onion: 1, thinly sliced
- Garlic cloves: 2, minced
- Fresh ginger: 1 1-inch piece, minced (or 1 tsp ground ginger)
- Soy sauce: 2 tbsp low sodium (or tamari for gluten-free)
- Rice vinegar or apple cider vinegar: 1 tbsp
- Sesame oil: 1 tbsp
- Cornstarch: 1 tbsp (optional, to thicken)
- Water: ¼ cup
- Black pepper: ½ tsp
- Red chili flakes: ¼ tsp (optional)
- Sesame seeds (for garnish, optional)
- Fresh cilantro or green onions (for garnish)

Instructions:

1. Slice the chicken breast into thin strips and season with black pepper. Set aside.
2. In a small bowl, whisk together the soy sauce, vinegar, sesame oil, minced garlic, ginger, and cornstarch (if using). Set aside.
3. Heat 1 tablespoon of olive oil in a large skillet or wok over medium-high heat. Add the chicken strips and saute for about 4-5 minutes until golden brown and cooked through. Remove the chicken from the skillet and set aside.
4. In the same skillet, heat the remaining tablespoon of olive oil.
5. Add the sliced onion and saute for 1-2 minutes until softened. Add the bell pepper, zucchini, carrots, and broccoli and saute for about 5-7 minutes, until the vegetables are crisp-tender. If the vegetables are sticking, add a splash of water to help them steam.
6. Add the cooked chicken to the skillet with the vegetables.
7. Pour the prepared sauce over the mixture and stir to coat everything evenly.
8. Let it cook for another 2-3 minutes, stirring often, until the sauce has thickened slightly and everything is well combined.
9. Garnish with sesame seeds, fresh cilantro, or green onions, if desired. Serve immediately as is or with a healthy carbs option like brown rice, cauliflower rice, or quinoa.

Variants and substitutions:

Feel free to substitute your favorite vegetables like snap peas, mushrooms, or pak choi. Swap the chicken for shrimp, tofu, or lean turkey breast for variety.

Nutritional information (per serving): Calories: 280 kcal; Protein: 28g; Fiber: 3g; Fat: 15g; Sugar: 4g; Net Carbs: 12g; Cholesterol 75mg; Sodium 450mg.

Chicken and Barley Soup

Time: *10 min* ***Cook:*** *35 min* ***Servings****: 4*

Ingredients:

- Chicken breasts or thighs: 1 pound boneless and skinless, cubed
- Olive oil: 1 tbsp
- Small onion: 1, finely chopped
- Garlic: 2 cloves, minced
- Medium carrots: 2, peeled and sliced
- Celery stalks: 2, sliced
- Pearl barley: ½ cup (preferably hulled barley for added fiber)
- Low-sodium chicken broth: 6 cups
- Bay leaf: 1 leaf
- Dried thyme: 1 tsp
- Dried oregano: 1 tsp
- Black pepper: ½ tsp
- Low-sodium salt
- Baby spinach or kale: 1 cup (optional)
- Fresh parsley: 2 tbsp, chopped (optional for garnish)

Instructions:

1. Dice the chicken and season with a little pepper. Set aside.
2. Heat the olive oil in a large soup pot over medium heat.
3. Add the chopped onion, garlic, carrots, and celery. Saute for about 5-7 minutes, stirring occasionally, until the vegetables are soft and fragrant.
4. Set the vegetables aside and add the diced chicken to the pot. Saute the chicken pieces for about 3-4 minutes, turning occasionally.
5. Add the barley and lightly toast it with the chicken and vegetables for 1-2 minutes to bring out the flavor.
6. Pour in the chicken broth and add the bay leaf, thyme, oregano, and black pepper. Stir to combine.
7. Bring the soup to a boil, then reduce the heat to low and simmer for about 25 minutes, or until the barley is tender and the chicken is cooked through.
8. If using spinach or kale, add it in the last 2-3 minutes of cooking so that the greens wilt slightly without overcooking.
9. Taste the soup and adjust the seasoning as needed, adding salt or more pepper if needed. Ladle the soup into bowls and garnish with fresh parsley if desired.

Variants and substitutions:

Add your favorite non-starchy vegetables, like zucchini, green beans, or bell peppers, for added fiber and variety. Use leftover cooked chicken or roasted chicken to make this meal even quicker. Simply stir it into the soup in the last few minutes of cooking.

Nutritional information (per serving): Calories: 260 kcal; Protein: 30g; Fiber: 7g; Fat: 15g; Sugar: 5g; Net Carbs: 30g; Cholesterol 85mg; Sodium 300mg.

Tomato Basil Soup

Time: *10 min* ***Cook:*** *30 min* ***Servings****: 4*

Ingredients:

- Olive oil: 2 tbsp
- Medium yellow onion: 1, chopped
- Garlic: 3 cloves, minced
- Large carrot: 1, peeled and chopped
- Medium tomatoes: 6 (or 1 28-ounce can whole peeled tomatoes, no sugar added)
- Low-sodium vegetable broth (or water): 3 cups
- Fresh basil leaves: ¼ cup (for garnish)
- Dried oregano: 1 tsp
- Black pepper: 1 tsp
- Low-sodium salt, to taste (optional, based on dietary preferences)
- Plain Greek yogurt or unsweetened almond milk: ¼ cup (optional for creaminess)

Instructions:

1. In a large pot, heat the olive oil over medium heat, and add the chopped onion, garlic, and carrot. Saute for about 5-7 minutes, stirring occasionally, until the vegetables are softened and the onions are translucent.
2. If using fresh tomatoes, peel and roughly chop them.
3. If using canned tomatoes, simply open the can and pour the tomatoes (along with the juice) into the pot.
4. Add the tomatoes to the pot with the sauteed vegetables. Add the vegetable broth (or water), basil, oregano, and black pepper.
5. Bring the soup to a boil, then reduce the heat to low and simmer for about 20-25 minutes, until the carrots are fully cooked and soft.
6. Once the soup has simmered, carefully blend it until it is smooth. You can use an immersion blender directly in the pot or transfer the soup to a stand blender. Blend until it is smooth. Return the blended soup to the pot. If the soup seems too thick, add more vegetable broth or water to achieve the desired consistency.
7. For a creamy consistency, add Greek yogurt or unsweetened almond milk during the last few minutes of cooking. This step is optional, but it adds richness without the extra calories or carbs.
8. Taste the soup and adjust the seasoning with more pepper or a pinch of salt, if necessary. Ladle the soup into bowls and garnish with fresh basil leaves for extra flavor and presentation.

Variants and substitutions:

Add grilled chicken or shrimp for added protein, which is great for those managing diabetes. Swap the Greek yogurt for unsweetened coconut milk or almond milk for a dairy-free version that still provides a rich texture.

Nutritional information (per serving): Calories: 130 kcal; Protein: 5g; Fiber: 5g; Fat: 20g; Sugar: 8g; Net Carbs: 15g; Cholesterol 0g; Sodium 150mg.

Whole Wheat Pasta with Vegetables and Lean Protein

Time: *10 min* ***Cook:*** *30 min* ***Servings****: 4*

Ingredients:

- Whole wheat pasta: 8 ounces (penne, rotini, or spaghetti)
- Olive oil: 2 tbsp (or avocado oil)
- Medium onion: 1, finely chopped
- Garlic: 2 cloves, minced
- Medium zucchini: 1, diced
- Small bell pepper: 1, diced (any color)
- Cherries: 1 cup, halved
- Fresh spinach: 2 cups (or kale), roughly chopped
- Cooked chicken breast or tofu: 1 cup, diced (or lean turkey)
- Dried oregano: 1 tsp
- Dried basil: ½ tsp
- Chili flakes: ¼ tsp (optional)
- Ground black pepper: ¼ teaspoon
- Pinch of salt (optional or use low-sodium substitute)
- Parmesan cheese: ¼ cup (optional, or use parmesan low fat)

Instructions:

1. Bring a large pot of salted water to a boil. Add the whole wheat pasta and cook according to the package instructions (usually about 8-10 minutes), until al dente.
2. Drain the pasta and set aside.
3. Heat 1 tablespoon of olive oil in a large skillet over medium heat, add the diced onion and cook for 3-4 minutes until softened, then add the minced garlic and cook for another minute, being careful not to burn it.
4. Add the diced zucchini and bell pepper. Saute for 5-7 minutes until tender but still slightly crunchy.
5. Add the cherry tomatoes and cook for another 2-3 minutes until softened.
6. Add the chopped spinach (or kale) to the skillet and cook for 1-2 minutes until wilted.
7. Add the cooked chicken breast, tofu, or lean turkey, making sure they are evenly distributed and heated through.
8. Season with oregano, basil, red pepper flakes (optional), black pepper, and a pinch of salt (if using).
9. Add the cooked whole wheat pasta to the skillet with the vegetables and protein. Pour the remaining tablespoon of olive oil over the top and gently toss everything together.
10. If using parmesan, sprinkle it over the top and toss again to incorporate.
11. Serve and garnish with extra herbs (such as fresh basil or parsley) and a small sprinkle of parmesan, if desired.

Variations:

Replace whole wheat pasta with gluten-free pasta (for example, chickpea, lentil, or quinoa varieties) to accommodate gluten sensitivity. For a more intense flavor, you can add a small amount of marinara sauce or a light tomato-based sauce, making sure it is low in sugar and sodium.

Nutritional information (per serving): Calories: 350 kcal; Protein: 20g; Fiber: 6g; Fat: 10g; Sugar: 5g; Net Carbs: 24g; Cholesterol 50mg; Sodium 180mg.

Spicy Pumpkin Soup

Time: *10 min* ***Cook:*** *30 min* ***Servings****: 4*

Ingredients:

- Olive oil: 2 tbsp (or avocado oil)
- Onion: 1 medium, finely chopped
- Garlic: 3 cloves, minced
- Pumpkin puree: 2 cups (unsweetened, canned or fresh)
- Vegetable or chicken broth: 4 cups (low sodium)
- Coconut milk: ½ cup (unsweetened, whole for creaminess or light for fewer calories)
- Chili powder: 1 tsp
- Cumin powder: 1 tsp
- Cinnamon powder: ½ tsp
- Turmeric powder: ½ tsp (optional for added anti-inflammatory benefits)
- Fresh ginger: 1 tsp, grated (or ½ tsp ground ginger)
- Cayenne pepper: ¼ teaspoon (optional for spiciness)
- Fresh cilantro: ¼ cup, chopped (for garnish)
- Greek yogurt (optional): ¼ cup, for garnish (use unsweetened yogurt)
- Salt: to taste (use sparingly for diabetes management)
- Black pepper: to taste
- Pumpkin seeds (optional): 2 tbsp, toasted, for garnish

Instructions:

1. Heat 2 tablespoons of olive oil in a large saucepan over medium heat, add the chopped onion and saute for 4-5 minutes until softened and translucent. Add the minced garlic and grated ginger and cook for another 1-2 minutes until fragrant, being careful not to burn them. Add and stir in the chili powder, ground cumin, cinnamon, turmeric (if using) and cayenne pepper. Cook the spices for 1 minute to release their flavors.
2. Add the pumpkin puree and broth to the saucepan. Stir well to combine all the ingredients. Bring the mixture to a boil over medium heat. Simmer for about 20 minutes, stirring occasionally. This will allow the flavors to meld together. If the soup becomes too thick, you can add a little more broth or water to adjust the consistency.
3. Once the soup has simmered and the flavors have developed, add the coconut milk for a creamy consistency. Continue cooking for another 5 minutes.
4. Taste the soup and season with salt and black pepper to taste. Ladle the soup into bowls and garnish with chopped fresh cilantro, a spoonful of Greek yogurt (optional), and toasted pumpkin seeds for extra crunch.

Variants and substitutions:

Use coconut yogurt or omit the yogurt entirely as a garnish. Make sure the broth is plant-based for a vegan version. Replace the full-fat coconut milk with light coconut milk or almond milk for a lighter version.

Nutritional information (per serving): Calories: 180 kcal; Protein: 5g; Fiber: 6g; Fat: 20g; Sugar: 5g; Net Carbs: 1g; Cholesterol 0g; Sodium 300mg.

No-Bake Almond Butter Balls

Time: *30 min* ***Servings****: 4*

Ingredients:

- Almond butter: ½ cup (unsweetened, natural)
- Oatmeal: ½ cup (use gluten-free oats if necessary)
- Ground flax seed: 2 tbsp
- Almond flour: ¼ cup
- Unsweetened shredded coconut: ¼ cup (optional)
- Chia seeds: 1 tbsp (optional, for added fiber and omega-3s)
- Unsweetened maple syrup: 2 tbsp (or similar sugar-free liquid sweetener)
- Vanilla extract: 1 tsp
- Low-sodium salt: a pinch (optional)

Instructions:

1. In a medium bowl, combine the almond butter, maple syrup, and vanilla extract. Mix well until smooth and fully combined.
2. Add the rolled oats, ground flax seed, almond flour, shredded coconut (if using), and chia seeds (if using). Mix until well combined. It should be sticky but firm enough to roll into balls. If it's too dry, add a little more almond butter; if it's too wet, add a little more almond flour or oats.
3. Using your hands, roll the mixture into small balls, about 1 inch in diameter. You should be able to make about 12-16 balls, depending on the size.
4. Place the almond butter balls on a parchment-lined plate or tray and refrigerate for about 20 minutes to firm up.
5. Once cooled, the almond butter balls are ready to eat. You can store them in an airtight container in the refrigerator for up to a week.

Variants and substitutions:

Replace the oats with 2 more tablespoons of almond flour and use a sugar-free sweetener like erythritol or stevia to further reduce the carbs. Replace the almond butter with sunflower seed butter to make this recipe nut-free. Add a pinch of cinnamon or cocoa powder for a different flavor profile. A sprinkle of sea salt on top before chilling also adds a great flavor contrast.

Nutritional information (per serving): Calories: 230 kcal; Protein: 6g; Fiber: 10g; Fat: 17g; Sugar: 1g; Net Carbs: 8g; Cholesterol 0g; Sodium 0g.

Baked Cinnamon Apples

Time: *10 min* ***Cook:*** *20 min* ***Servings****: 4*

Ingredients:

- Apples: 4 medium (Granny Smith or Fuji)
- Cinnamon powder: 1 ½ tsp
- Nutmeg powder: ¼ tsp
- Ginger powder: ¼ tsp (optional)
- Vanilla extract: 1 tsp
- Unsweetened applesauce: 2 tbsp (or water)
- Unsweetened almond flour or chopped walnuts: 2 tsp (optional for crunch)
- Unsweetened maple syrup: 2 tbsp (or monk fruit sweetener or stevia)
- Butter: 1 tbsp
- Lemon juice: 1 tbsp
- Low-sodium salt: a pinch

Instructions:

1. Set the oven temperature to 375°F (190°C).
2. Wash the apples and cut them in half. Use a spoon to remove the core and seeds, creating a small well in the center. Place the apple halves, skin side down, on a baking sheet.
3. In a small bowl, combine the ground cinnamon, nutmeg, ginger (if using), a pinch of salt, and your favorite sweetener. Add the vanilla extract and apple juice or water to form a paste.
4. Spread the spice mixture evenly into the wells of each apple half. If desired, sprinkle the tops with almond meal or chopped walnuts for texture and fiber.
5. Dot the apples with small pats of butter (or non-dairy butter). Drizzle the apples with lemon juice for flavor.
6. Cover the baking sheet with aluminum foil and bake for 15 to 20 minutes, or until the apples are tender but hold their shape. Remove the foil during the last 5 minutes of cooking to lightly brown the surface.
7. Once cooked, let the apples cool slightly before serving.

Variants and substitutions:

Use non-dairy butter or coconut oil instead of regular butter. Serve with a side of unsweetened Greek yogurt mixed with a little cinnamon and vanilla extract to round out the flavors.

Nutritional information (per serving): Calories: 130 kcal; Protein: 1g; Fiber: 10g; Fat: 4g; Sugar: 35g; Net Carbs: 18g; Cholesterol 5 mg (less with vegetable butter); Sodium 40mg.

Sugar-Free Lemon Cheescake

***Time:** 30 min* ***Servings**: 4*

Ingredients:

- Cream cheese: 8 ounces, softened (use dairy-free cream cheese if necessary)
- Greek yogurt: ¼ cup (unsweetened or use dairy-free yogurt)
- Lemon juice: 2 tbsp (freshly squeezed)
- Lemon zest: 1 tsp (from 1 lemon)
- Sugar-free sweetener: ¼ cup (erythritol, monk fruit, or stevia)
- Vanilla extract: ½ tsp
- Egg: 1 large

Topping (optional):

- Fresh berries: ¼ cup (such as blueberries, raspberries or strawberries)
- Lemon zest: for garnish

Instructions:

1. In a bowl, beat the softened cream cheese until smooth and creamy.
2. Add the Greek yogurt, lemon juice, lemon zest, sugar-free sweetener, and vanilla extract. Continue to beat until combined.
3. Beat the egg until smooth and fully incorporated.
4. Pour the filling directly into the pan or ramekins.
5. Smooth the tops with the back of a spoon.
6. Cover the cheesecakes with plastic wrap and refrigerate for at least 20 minutes to firm up. For a firmer texture, you can refrigerate them longer.
7. Garnish with fresh berries and a sprinkle of lemon zest for extra sparkle. Enjoy immediately or refrigerate until ready to serve.

Variants and substitutions:

Add 1 teaspoon of ground cinnamon or a drop of almond extract to the filling for a different flavor profile. You can also add a handful of fresh blueberries or raspberries before chilling. For a vegan version, use a dairy-free cream cheese and Greek yogurt substitute (such as almond or coconut alternatives) and replace the egg with a flax egg.

Nutritional information (per serving): Calories: 220 kcal; Protein: 7g; Fiber: 2g; Fat: 19g; Sugar: 1g; Net Carbs: 4g; Cholesterol 50mg; Sodium 150mg.

Avocado Chocolate Mousse

Time: *25 min* ***Servings****: 4*

Ingredients:

- Ripe avocados: 2 medium
- Unsweetened cocoa powder: ¼ cup
- Unsweetened sweetener: ¼ cup (erythritol, monk fruit, or stevia)
- Unsweetened almond milk: ¼ cup (or any low-carbs milk alternative like coconut milk or cashew milk)
- Vanilla extract: 1 tsp
- Lemon or lime juice: 1 tsp (optional, for extra flavor)
- Pinch of salt
- Unsweetened dark chocolate chips: 2 tbsp (optional, for extra richness)

Instructions:

1. Cut and hollow out the avocado, discarding the pit and skin. Place the avocado in a food processor or high-powered blender.
2. Add the unsweetened cocoa powder, sugar-free sweetener, almond milk, vanilla extract, lemon or lime juice (if using), and a pinch of salt to the blender.
3. Blend the mixture for 1-2 minutes until completely smooth and creamy. If the mousse is too thick, you can add a tablespoon of almond milk at a time until you reach the desired consistency.
4. Optional: Melt the chocolate chips:
5. For a more intense flavor, melt the sugar-free dark chocolate chips in the microwave in 30-second intervals, stirring occasionally, or melt them in a double boiler. Once melted, add them to the mousse mixture.
6. Divide the mousse evenly among 4 small serving bowls and refrigerate for at least 15 minutes to allow it to firm up slightly. You can also serve it immediately if you prefer a softer consistency.
7. Garnish with optional toppings such as sugar-free whipped cream, fresh berries, or a sprinkling of shredded coconut for added texture and flavor.

Variants and substitutions:

Add a teaspoon of instant espresso powder for a mocha flavor, or a pinch of cayenne pepper for a spicy chocolate mousse. For an extra creamy mousse, you can add a couple of tablespoons of coconut cream or Greek yogurt (use dairy-free if necessary).

Nutritional information (per serving): Calories: 180 kcal; Protein: 3g; Fiber: 20g; Fat: 16g (from avocado); Sugar: 1g; Net Carbs: 4g; Cholesterol: 0g; Sodium: 40mg.

Raspberry Coconut Bars

Time: *10 min* ***Cook:*** *15 min* ***Servings****: 4*

Ingredients:

Crust:

- Almond flour: ½ cup
- Coconut flour: 2 tbsp
- Sugar-free sweetener: 2 tbsp (such as erythritol or monk fruit)
- Coconut oil: 2 tbsp, melted (or butter)
- Vanilla extract: ½ tsp

Filling:

- Fresh or frozen raspberries: ½ cup (unsweetened)
- Unsweetened shredded coconut: ¼ cup
- Sugar-free sweetener: 1-2 tbsp (to taste, depending on the sweetness of the raspberries)
- Chia seeds: 1 tsp (optional, for added fiber)
- Coconut milk: 2 tbsp (unsweetened, canned or carton)
- Lemon juice: 1 tsp (optional)

Topping:

- Unsweetened shredded coconut: 2 tbsp
- Unsweetened dark chocolate chips: 2 tbsp, melted (optional)

Instructions:

1. Set the oven temperature to 350°F (175°C). In a medium bowl, combine the almond flour, coconut flour, sweetener, melted coconut oil (or butter), and vanilla extract. Mix until the mixture resembles crumbly dough.
2. Line a small 8x8-inch baking pan with parchment paper. Press the dough evenly into the bottom of the pan. Bake until the edges are lightly browned, 8 to 10 minutes. Remove from the oven and let cool slightly.
3. In a small saucepan over medium heat, add the raspberries, shredded coconut, sweetener, and chia seeds (if using). Add the coconut milk and lemon juice. Bake, stirring occasionally, until the raspberries are broken down and the mixture is slightly thickened, about 5 minutes.
4. Spread the raspberry-coconut filling evenly over the cooled crust. Sprinkle the tops with additional shredded coconut for a crunchy texture. Return the pan to the oven and bake for an additional 7-8 minutes to firm up the filling.
5. Let the bars cool completely before cutting into 4 even squares. If desired, drizzle melted sugar-free dark chocolate over the bars for an extra indulgent touch.
6. Serve the Raspberry Coconut Bars cold or at room temperature. They can be refrigerated for up to 3 days.

Variants and substitutions:

Use a sugar-free vegan sweetener, and make sure any optional toppings like chocolate chips are dairy-free. Make sure all sweeteners and ingredients used are keto-approved, and consider adding extra chia seeds for a higher fiber content.

Nutritional information (per serving): Calories: kcal; Protein: 5g; Fiber: 6g; Fat: 17 g (healthy fats from coconut flour and almonds); Sugar: 3g; Net Carbs: 6g; Cholesterol 20mg; Sodium 0g.

Turmeric Milk (Golden Milk)

Time: *5 min* ***Cook:*** *5 min* ***Serving****: 1*

Ingredients:

- Unsweetened almond milk (or any other plant-based milk): 1 cup
- Turmeric powder: ½ tsp
- Cinnamon powder: ¼ tsp
- Ginger powder: ¼ tsp
- Black pepper: a pinch
- Sugar-free sweetener: 1 tsp (optional, such as stevia or monk fruit)
- Vanilla extract: ¼ tsp (optional, for extra flavor)
- Coconut oil or ghee: ½ tsp (optional)

Instructions:

1. In a small saucepan, heat the almond milk over medium heat until it begins to steam but not boil.
2. Add the turmeric powder, cinnamon, ginger and a pinch of black pepper. Whisk well to combine the spices with the milk. If using, add the vanilla extract and coconut oil/ghee at this stage.
3. Let the mixture simmer for 3-5 minutes to infuse the flavors. Stir occasionally to prevent the spices from clumping.
4. Remove from the heat and add your sugar-free sweetener, adjusting the sweetness to your liking.
5. If you prefer a smoother consistency, you can strain the golden milk to remove any bits of spice that haven't fully dissolved.
6. Pour the turmeric milk into your favorite mug and enjoy warm. For an extra touch, sprinkle a pinch of cinnamon on top before serving.

Variants and substitutions:

If you don't have or prefer almond milk, use unsweetened coconut milk, oat milk, or soy milk. For a creamier version, you can use canned full-fat coconut milk. To make it more satisfying, add a scoop of unflavored or vanilla-flavored protein powder, which is low in carbs and sugar.

Nutritional information (per serving): Calories: 60 kcal; Protein: Negligible; Fiber: 1g; Fat: Negligible; Sugar: Negligible; Net Carbs: 1g; Cholesterol 0g; Sodium 150mg.

Sugar-Free Berry Smoothie

Time: *5 min* ***Serving****: 1*

Ingredients:

- Unsweetened almond milk (or any low-carb milk alternative): ½ cup
- Greek yogurt (unsweetened, plain or vanilla, low-fat or whole): ¼ cup
- Mixed berries (frozen or fresh; blueberries, strawberries, raspberries): ½ cup
- Chia seeds: 1 tbsp (optional)
- Ground flax seed: 1 tbsp (optional for fiber and omega-3s)
- Vanilla extract: ¼ tsp (optional)
- Ice cubes: 4-5 (optional if using fresh berries)
- Sugar-free sweetener: 1-2 tsp (optional, such as stevia, monk fruit, or erythritol, to taste)

Instructions:

1. If using fresh berries, you can add a few ice cubes for a thick, cold consistency. Frozen berries can be used straight without ice.
2. In a blender, combine the almond milk, Greek yogurt, mixed berries, chia seeds, ground flax seed, vanilla extract, and sweetener (if using). Blend on high for about 30-45 seconds until smooth and creamy.
3. If the smoothie is too thick, you can add a little more almond milk. For a thicker consistency, add a few more ice cubes or more frozen berries.
4. Strain into a glass and enjoy immediately. You can garnish with a few whole berries or a sprinkle of chia seeds on top, if desired.

Variants and substitutions:

In place of almond milk, you can use unsweetened coconut milk, soy milk, or any low-carbs milk alternative. Cow's milk works too, but opt for skim or semi-skim to keep the calories low. You can substitute coconut yogurt or any non-dairy yogurt for the Greek yogurt to make it dairy-free. Choose a low-sugar or sugar-free variety for best results. Add a pinch of cinnamon, nutmeg, or a tablespoon of unsweetened cocoa powder for added depth of flavor.

Nutritional information (per serving): Calories: 150 kcal; Protein: 7g; Fiber: 3g; Fat: 4g; Sugar: 10g; Net Carbs: 0g; Cholesterol 0g; Sodium 80mg.

Herbal Iced Tea with Lemon and Mint

Time: *15 min* ***Cook:*** *10 min* ***Serving****: 1*

Ingredients:

- Water: 1 cup (strained)
- Herbal tea bag (chamomile, peppermint, or any non-caffeinated blend): 1
- Fresh mint leaves: 4-6 leaves, plus more for garnish
- Fresh lemon juice: 1 tbsp (from about ½ lemon)
- Lemon slices: 1-2 slices (for garnish)
- Ice cubes: 5-6
- Optional sweetener: stevia, monk fruit, or erythritol to taste

Instructions:

1. In a small saucepan, bring 1 cup of filtered water to a boil.
2. Once the water reaches a boil, remove from the heat and add the tea bag and mint leaves to the hot water. Let steep for 5 to 7 minutes to extract the flavors.
3. After steeping, remove the tea bag and mint leaves. Let the tea cool to room temperature for about 10 minutes or speed up the process by placing it in the refrigerator for 5 to 10 minutes.
4. Once the tea has cooled, add the fresh lemon juice. Taste and adjust the acidity; you can add more lemon if desired.
5. If you prefer a sweeter iced tea, add a sugar-free sweetener such as stevia or monk fruit to taste. Stir well to dissolve.
6. Fill a glass with ice cubes and pour the cooled tea over the ice. Garnish with a lemon wedge and a few mint leaves.

Variants and substitutions:

Try using hibiscus, rooibos, or ginger tea for a different flavor profile. Hibiscus adds a beautiful red color, and ginger adds a warm, spicy kick. Swap the lemon juice for lime juice or a lemon-orange combination for a citrus twist. For an added kick, freeze lemon- or mint-infused ice cubes to enhance the flavor of your tea as it melts.

Nutritional information (per serving): Calories: 5 kcal; Protein: Negligible; Fiber: Negligible; Fat: Negligible; Sugar: 1g; Net Carbs: 1g; Cholesterol 0g; Sodium 0g.

Spicy Apple Cider Vinegar Drink

Time: *5 min* ***Cook:*** *5 min* ***Serving****: 1*

Ingredients:

- Apple Cider Vinegar: 1 tbsp (organic, raw, unfiltered)
- Water: 1 cup (filtered, warm or room temperature)
- Cinnamon Powder: ¼ tsp
- Ginger Powder: ¼ tsp (optional)
- Fresh Lemon Juice: 1 tsp (optional)
- Sugar-Free Sweetener: Stevia, Monk Fruit, or Erythritol to taste
- Ice Cubes: Optional (if served cold)
- Apple Slices or Cinnamon Stick: For Garnish (optional)

Instructions:

1. For a spicy hot drink, heat 1 cup of water until hot but not boiling. Alternatively, use room temperature or cold water for an iced version.
2. In a glass, add 1 tablespoon of apple cider vinegar. Add the ground cinnamon and ginger (if using). Add fresh lemon juice for extra zesty flavor.
3. Add your favorite sugar-free sweetener, such as stevia or monk fruit, to taste. Start with a small amount and adjust to taste.
4. Pour the hot or cold water over the vinegar and spices and stir well until fully combined.
5. If serving cold, add a few ice cubes. Garnish with an apple slice or cinnamon stick for a decorative and flavorful touch.

Variants and substitutions:

Replace the water with a cold herbal tea, such as chamomile or ginger tea, for an extra layer of flavor. Add a few slices of fresh berries (like raspberries or strawberries) or apple slices to infuse the drink with a more natural sweetness and fruitiness. Replace the lemon juice with lime juice or add orange zest for a citrusy twist.

Nutritional information (per serving): Calories: 5 kcal; Protein: 0g; Fiber: 0g; Fat: 0g Sugar: 0g; Net Carbs: 1g; Cholesterol 0g; Sodium 0g.

Homemade Almond Milk

Time: *10 min* ***Serving****: 1*

Ingredients:

- Raw Almonds: ¼ cup (soaked 6-8 hours or overnight, optional for a creamier consistency)
- Water: 1 cup (strained)
- Vanilla Extract: ¼ tsp (optional)
- Cinnamon: 1 pinch (optional)
- Sugar-Free Sweetener: Stevia, Monk Fruit, or Erythritol to taste (optional)

Instructions:

1. For a creamier almond milk, soak ¼ cup raw almonds in water for 6 to 8 hours or overnight. Drain and rinse the almonds before using. If you're in a hurry, you can skip this step, but the milk will be a little less creamy.
2. Add the soaked (or unsoaked) almonds to a high-speed blender with 1 cup filtered water. Blend on high for 1 to 2 minutes, or until the almonds are completely broken down and the mixture looks creamy.
3. Using a nut milk bag, cheesecloth, or fine-mesh strainer, strain the almond milk into a bowl or large glass. Squeeze out as much of the liquid as possible, leaving the almond meat.
4. For additional flavor, add ¼ teaspoon vanilla extract and a pinch of cinnamon. For a hint of sweetness, add a few drops of a sugar-free sweetener like stevia or monk fruit.
5. Pour almond milk into a glass or jar. It can be served immediately or chilled in the refrigerator for later. Shake before each use, as natural separation may occur.

Variants and substitutions:

Swap out the almonds for sunflower seeds or hemp seeds to make a seed milk for those with nut allergies. For a warmer flavor, add ¼ teaspoon ground turmeric and a pinch of black pepper to the milk for an anti-inflammatory kick. Blend a few fresh or frozen berries into the almond milk for a fruity, antioxidant-rich version.

Nutritional information (per serving): Calories: 40 kcal; Fiber: 1g; Fat: 4g; Sugar: Negligible; Net Carbs: 1g; Cholesterol: 0g; Sodium: 0g.

Roasted Garlic Cauliflower

Time: *5 min* ***Cook:*** *20 min* ***Serving****: 1*

Ingredients:

- Cauliflower florets: 1 cup (about ¼ of a medium head)
- Olive oil: 1 tbsp (or avocado oil)
- Garlic cloves: 2, minced
- Salt: ¼ tsp (or to taste)
- Black pepper: ¼ tsp (or to taste)
- Smoked paprika: ¼ tsp (optional)
- Fresh parsley: 1 tbsp, minced (optional garnish)
- Lemon juice: 1 tsp (optional)

Instructions:

1. Set the oven temperature to 425°F (220°C).
2. Wash and cut the cauliflower into bite-sized florets. Pat them dry with a paper towel to help them roast more evenly.
3. In a large bowl, toss the cauliflower florets with the olive oil, minced garlic, salt, pepper, and smoked paprika (if using). Make sure the cauliflower is well coated.
4. Spread the seasoned cauliflower in a single layer on a baking sheet. Roast in the pre-heated oven for 20 minutes, turning halfway through, until the cauliflower is golden brown and tender.
5. Once roasted, remove the cauliflower from the oven. If desired, sprinkle with chopped fresh parsley and a squeeze of lemon juice for extra gloss.
6. Serve the Garlic Roasted Cauliflower warm as a side dish or as a light meal. You can pair it with a protein like grilled chicken or fish for a more substantial meal.

Variants and substitutions:

Add ¼ teaspoon red pepper flakes or cayenne pepper for a spicy kick. Sprinkle 1 tablespoon grated Parmesan cheese or a dairy-free alternative over the cauliflower during the last 5 minutes of cooking for a cheesy flavor. If parsley is not available, use fresh cilantro or basil as a garnish.

Nutritional information (per serving): Calories: 120 kcal; Protein: 2g; Fiber: 8g; Fat: 24g; Sugar: Negligible; Net Carbs: 4g; Cholesterol: 0g; Sodium: 300mg.

Sauteed Green Beans with Almonds

Time: *10 min* ***Cook:*** *10 min* ***Serving****: 1*

Ingredients:

- Fresh Green Beans: 1 cup (chopped)
- Olive Oil: 1 tbsp (or avocado oil)
- Garlic Cloves: 2, thinly sliced or minced
- Sliced Almonds: 1 tbsp (unsalted)
- Lemon Juice: 1 tsp (optional)
- Salt: ¼ tsp (or to taste)
- Black Pepper: ¼ tsp (or to taste)
- Red Chili Flakes: 1 pinch (optional)

Instructions:

1. Bring a pot of salted water to a boil. Add the green beans and blanch for 2 to 3 minutes, until bright green and slightly tender but still crunchy. Drain the green beans and immediately transfer them to a bowl of ice water to stop the cooking process. Drain and pat dry.
2. While the green beans blanch, heat a dry skillet over medium heat. Add the sliced almonds and toast, stirring frequently, for 2 to 3 minutes until golden and fragrant. Remove from the skillet and set aside.
3. In the same skillet, add 1 tablespoon of olive oil over medium heat. Add the sliced or minced garlic and saute for about 1 minute until fragrant, being careful not to burn it.
4. Add the blanched green beans to the skillet with the garlic. Stir to coat with the garlic and oil, then cook for a further 3-4 minutes, stirring occasionally, until the beans are tender but slightly crisp.
5. Add the toasted almonds to the pan and stir to combine. Season with salt, black pepper and red chilli flakes (if using). If desired, drizzle with a teaspoon of lemon juice for a fresh, tangy finish.
6. Serve the sauteed green beans warm as a side dish or a light main course. They pair well with roast meats, grilled fish or a simple grain bowl.

Variants and substitutions:

Swap the almonds for pumpkin seeds or sunflower seeds for a nut-free version that retains the crunch. For more variety, sauté sliced bell peppers or cherry tomatoes with the green beans for added color and flavor. Swap the olive oil for avocado oil or ghee for a different flavor or to accommodate specific dietary preferences.

Nutritional information (per serving): Calories: 170 kcal; Protein: 3g; Fiber: 7g; Fat: 14g; Sugar: 3g; Net Carbs: 6g; Cholesterol: 0g; Sodium: 180mg.

Zucchini and Tomato Gratin

Time: *10 min* ***Cook:*** *20 min* ***Serving****: 1*

Ingredients:

- Zucchini: 1 medium, thinly sliced
- Tomato: 1 medium, thinly sliced
- Olive oil: 1 tbsp (or avocado oil)
- Garlic: 1 clove, minced
- Parmesan cheese: 2 tbsp, grated (or nutritional yeast for a vegan option)
- Mozzarella cheese: 2 tbsp, grated (use a lean or plant-based variety if you prefer)
- Whole-wheat breadcrumbs: 1 tbsp (or gluten-free breadcrumbs for gluten sensitivity)
- Fresh basil: 1 tbsp, chopped (optional)
- Salt: ¼ tsp
- Black pepper: ¼ tsp

Instructions:

1. Set the oven temperature to 400°F (200°C) and lightly grease a small baking sheet with olive oil or cooking spray.
2. In a small skillet, heat 1 tablespoon of the olive oil over medium heat. Add the minced garlic and saute for about 1 minute until fragrant. Remove from heat and set aside.
3. In the greased baking sheet, arrange alternating layers of zucchini and tomato slices. Season each layer with a pinch of salt and black pepper. Drizzle the sauteed garlic and olive oil mixture evenly over the top.
4. Sprinkle the grated Parmesan and shredded mozzarella over the layered vegetables. Then, add breadcrumbs to the top for a crunchy texture. If using fresh basil, sprinkle it over the baking sheet before adding the cheese.
5. Place the pan in the preheated oven and bake for 15 to 20 minutes, or until the cheese is melted and golden brown, and the zucchini is tender but not mushy.
6. Remove from the oven and let cool for a minute or two before serving. This gratin can be enjoyed on its own or as a side dish with a lean protein like grilled chicken or fish.

Variants and substitutions:

Swap Parmesan and mozzarella for plant-based cheeses or nutritional yeast to keep it vegan and dairy-free. Swap whole wheat breadcrumbs for gluten-free breadcrumbs or chopped almonds for added texture. Add thin slices of eggplant or bell peppers to add variety and color to the dish.

Nutritional information (per serving): Calories: 180 kcal; Protein: 8g; Fiber: 3g; Fat: 12g; Sugar: 5g; Net Carbs: 7g.; Cholesterol: 0g; Sodium: 320mg.

Spicy Roasted Chickpeas

Time: *10 min* ***Cook:*** *25 min* ***Serving****: 1*

Ingredients:

- Canned Chickpeas: ½ cup, drained and rinsed
- Olive Oil: ½ tbsp (or avocado oil)
- Smoked Paprika: ¼ tsp
- Cayenne Pepper: ¼ tsp (adjust to taste)
- Garlic Powder: ¼ tsp
- Ground Cumin: ¼ tsp
- Salt: ¼ teaspoon (optional or adjust to taste)
- Black Pepper: pinch
- Fresh Lemon Juice: optional, for garnish

Instructions:

1. Set the oven temperature to 400°F (200°C). Line a baking sheet with parchment paper for easy cleanup.
2. Drain and rinse the canned chickpeas thoroughly, then pat them dry with a paper towel. Removing as much moisture as possible will help the chickpeas crisp up nicely in the oven.
3. In a medium bowl, toss the dried chickpeas with the olive oil, smoked paprika, cayenne, garlic powder, ground cumin, salt, and black pepper until evenly coated.
4. Spread the seasoned chickpeas in an even layer on the prepared baking sheet. Roast in the preheated oven for 20 to 25 minutes, shaking the sheet halfway through to ensure even roasting. The chickpeas should be crispy and golden brown.
5. Once roasted, remove from the oven and let cool for a minute. Optionally, drizzle with fresh lemon juice for a tangy finish. Enjoy as a snack or as a crunchy addition to salads or cereal bowls.

Variants and substitutions:

If you prefer a milder flavor, reduce or omit the cayenne pepper and increase the smoked paprika for a smoky but less spicy version. Replace the spices with ½ teaspoon dried herbs like rosemary or thyme for a savory, herbal snack. For an oil-free version, use a splash of vegetable broth to coat the chickpeas before adding the spices. The chickpeas may be slightly less crunchy, but still flavorful.

Nutritional information (per serving): Calories: 130 kcal; Protein: 5g; Fiber: 7g; Fat: 10g; Sugar: 1g; Net Carb 12g; Cholesterol: 0g; Sodium: 200 mg.

Butternut Squash Puree

Time:* 5** *min* ***Cook: *25 min* ***Serving****: 1*

Ingredients:

- Butternut squash: 1 cup, peeled, cubed (about ½ small squash)
- Olive oil: ½ tbsp (or avocado oil)
- Garlic: 1 clove, minced
- Ground cinnamon: ¼ tsp (optional)
- Salt: pinch (optional, to taste)
- Ground black pepper: pinch
- Unsweetened almond milk: ¼ cup (optional for a creamier consistency)

Instructions:

1. Peel and dice the butternut squash into 1-inch pieces. The smaller the pieces, the faster they will cook.
2. Place the cubed butternut squash in a steamer basket over a pot of boiling water, cover, and steam for about 15 to 20 minutes until the squash is tender. Alternatively, you can boil the squash in a pot of water for the same amount of time.
3. While the squash is cooking, heat the olive oil in a small skillet over medium heat. Add the minced garlic and saute for about 1 minute, until fragrant but not browned.
4. Transfer the cooked squash to a blender or food processor. Add the sauteed garlic, a pinch of salt, pepper, and cinnamon (if using). Blend until smooth. For a creamier consistency, slowly add the almond milk as you blend.
5. Taste the puree and adjust seasoning if necessary. Add more salt, pepper, or cinnamon to taste.
6. Serve warm butternut squash puree as a side dish, or use it as a base for grain bowls or as a garnish for roasted meats or vegetables.

Variants and substitutions:

Add a pinch of ground nutmeg, allspice, or ginger for a spicier flavor, perfect for fall or holiday meals. This recipe is naturally vegan, but for an extra creamy, dairy-free texture, add coconut milk instead of almond milk.

Nutritional information (per serving): Calories: 140 kcal; Fiber: 6g; Fat: 7g; Protein: 2g; Sugar: 4g; Net Carbs: 16g; Cholesterol: 0,1g; Sodium: 60mg.

Almond Flour Bread

Time: *10 min* ***Cook:*** *25 min* ***Serving****: 1 loaf (about 12 slices)*

Ingredients:

- Almond flour: 2 cups (fine almond flour works best)
- Baking powder: 1 tbsp (make sure it is aluminum-free)
- Eggs: 4 large
- Olive oil: 2 tbsp (or avocado oil)
- Unsweetened almond milk: ¼ cup (or any unsweetened plant-based milk)
- Salt: ½ tsp
- Apple cider vinegar: 1 tsp (for extra fluffiness)

Instructions:

1. Set the oven temperature to 350°F (175°C). Grease a 9x5-inch loaf pan or line it with parchment paper to prevent sticking.
2. In a large bowl, whisk together the almond flour, baking powder, and salt until well combined. Make sure there are no lumps in the flour.
3. In a separate bowl, whisk together the eggs, olive oil, unsweetened almond milk, and apple cider vinegar until smooth.
4. Gradually add the wet ingredients to the dry, stirring until a thick, smooth batter forms.
5. Pour the batter into the prepared loaf pan and smooth the top with a spatula.
6. Bake in the preheated oven for 25 to 30 minutes, or until the top is golden brown and a toothpick inserted into the center comes out clean.
7. Let the bread cool in the pan for 10 minutes before transferring to a wire rack to cool completely.

Variants and substitutions:

Add 1-2 teaspoons of dried herbs like rosemary, thyme, or oregano to the dry ingredients for a flavorful kick. For a sweeter bread, add 1-2 tablespoons of a low-carb sweetener like monk fruit or erythritol and a pinch of cinnamon.

Nutritional information (per serving): Calories: 140 kcal; Fiber: 2g; Fat: 15g; Protein: 6g; Sugar: 1; Net Carbs 2g; Cholesterol: 0,8g; Sodium: 120mg.

Coconut Flour Bread

Time: *10 min* ***Cook:*** *20 min* ***Serving****: 1 loaf (about 12 slices)*

Ingredients:

- Coconut flour: 1 cup
- Baking powder: 1 tbsp (make sure it doesn't contain aluminum)
- Eggs: 4 large
- Olive oil: ¼ cup (or melted coconut oil)
- Unsweetened almond milk: ¼ cup (or any unsweetened plant-based milk)
- Low-sodium salt: ½ tsp
- Honey or low-carb sweetener: 1 tbsp (optional, can be omitted for a savory bread)

Instructions:

1. Set the oven temperature to 350°F (175°C). Grease a 9x5-inch loaf pan or line it with parchment paper to prevent sticking.
2. In a large bowl, whisk together the coconut flour, baking powder, and salt until well combined. Make sure there are no lumps in the flour.
3. In a separate bowl, whisk together the eggs, olive oil, almond milk, and honey (if using) until smooth and well combined.
4. Gradually add the wet ingredients to the dry, stirring until the batter is thick and smooth. The coconut flour will quickly absorb the moisture.
5. Pour the batter into the prepared loaf pan and smooth the top with a spatula.
6. Bake in the preheated oven for 20 to 25 minutes, or until the top is golden brown and a toothpick inserted into the center comes out clean.
7. Allow the bread to cool in the pan for 5-10 minutes before transferring to a wire rack to cool completely.

Variants and substitutions:

Add ½ cup shredded cheese and 1 tablespoon dried herbs (such as rosemary, thyme, or oregano) for a flavorful twist. Increase the sweetener to 2 tablespoons and add 1 teaspoon vanilla extract for a sweeter bread. You can also add ½ cup unsweetened shredded coconut.

Nutritional information (per serving): Calories: 120 kcal; Fiber: 3g; Fat: 9g; Protein: 5g; Sugar: 1g; Net Carbs 1g; Cholesterol: 1,3g; Sodium: 100mg.

Flax Seed Bread

Time: *10 min* ***Cook:*** *20 min* ***Serving****: 1 loaf (about 12 slices)*

Ingredients:

- Ground flax seed: 1 cup (flax seed meal)
- Almond flour: 1 cup (or sunflower meal for a nut-free version)
- Baking powder: 1 tbsp (aluminum-free)
- Low-sodium salt: ½ tsp
- Eggs: 4 large
- Water: ¼ cup (or unsweetened almond milk)
- Olive oil: 2 tbsp (or melted coconut oil)
- Optional sweetener: 1 tbsp honey or low-carbs sweetener (optional, for a slightly sweet bread)

Instructions:

1. Set the oven temperature to 350°F (175°C). Grease a 9x5-inch loaf pan or line it with parchment paper.
2. In a large bowl, combine the ground flax seed, almond flour, baking powder, and salt. Mix well to ensure everything is evenly distributed.
3. In a separate bowl, whisk together the eggs, water (or almond milk), and olive oil until fully combined.
4. Pour the wet ingredients into the dry ingredients and stir until a thick batter forms. The batter may be quite thick, which is normal.
5. Pour the batter into the prepared loaf pan, smoothing the top with a spatula.
6. Bake in the preheated oven for 20 to 25 minutes, or until the top is golden brown and a toothpick inserted into the center comes out clean.
7. Allow the bread to cool in the pan for 5-10 minutes before transferring to a wire rack to cool completely.

Variants and substitutions:

Add 1 teaspoon dried herbs (such as rosemary, thyme, or Italian seasoning) for a savory flavor. For a sweeter bread, increase the sweetener to 2 tablespoons and add 1 teaspoon vanilla extract or cinnamon.

Nutritional information (per serving): Calories: 100 kcal; Fiber: 4g; Fat: 7g; Protein: 5g; Sugar: 1g; Net Carbs 0g; Cholesterol: 0g; Sodium: 120mg.

Whole Wheat Oatmeal Bread

Time: *10 min* ***Cook:*** *20 min* ***Serving****: 1 loaf (about 12 slices)*

Ingredients:

- Whole wheat flour: 1 cup
- Oatmeal: 1 cup (can be made by blending rolled oats in a food processor)
- Baking powder: 2 tsp(aluminum-free)
- Baking soda: ½ tsp
- Salt: ½ tsp
- Honey: 2 tbsp (or maple syrup for a vegan option)
- Eggs: 2 large (or ½ cup unsweetened applesauce for a vegan option)
- Milk: 1 cup (or unsweetened almond milk for a dairy-free option)
- Olive oil: 2 tbsp (or melted coconut oil)

Instructions:

1. Set the oven temperature to 350°F (175°C). Grease a 9x5-inch loaf pan or line it with parchment paper.
2. In a large bowl, combine the whole wheat flour, oatmeal, baking powder, baking soda, and salt. Mix well to ensure even distribution.
3. In a separate bowl, whisk together the honey, eggs (or applesauce), milk (or almond milk), and olive oil until smooth.
4. Pour the wet mixture into the dry mixture and stir until combined. Be careful not to over-mix; a few lumps are okay.
5. Pour the batter into the prepared loaf pan, smoothing the top with a spatula.
6. Bake in the preheated oven for 20 to 25 minutes, or until the top is golden brown and a toothpick inserted into the center comes out clean.
7. Allow the bread to cool in the pan for 5-10 minutes before transferring to a wire rack to cool completely.

Variants and substitutions:

Add ½ cup chia seeds, sunflower seeds, or chopped walnuts for added texture and nutrition. Replace the eggs with ½ cup unsweetened applesauce and use almond milk. Use a gluten-free flour blend (like Bob's Red Mill 1-to-1) in place of the whole wheat flour, but be sure to adjust the liquid as needed.

Nutritional information (per serving): Calories: 120 kcal; Fiber: 3g; Net Carbs: 15g; Fat: 4g; Protein: 6g; Sugar: 2g; Cholesterol: 0g; Sodium: 130mg.

Chia Seed and Almond Bread

Time: *10 min* ***Cook:*** *20 min* ***Serving****: 1 loaf (about 12 slices)*

Ingredients:

- Almond flour: 2 cups
- Chia seeds: ¼ cup
- Baking powder: 1 tbsp (aluminum-free)
- Baking soda: ½ tsp
- Low-sodium salt: ½ tsp
- Eggs: 3 large
- Milk: 1 cup (or unsweetened almond milk for a dairy-free option)
- Olive oil: 2 tbsp (or melted coconut oil)
- Honey: 2 tbsp (or maple syrup for a vegan option)

Instructions:

1. Set the oven temperature to 350°F (175°C). Grease a 9x5-inch loaf pan or line it with parchment paper.
2. In a large bowl, combine the almond flour, chia seeds, baking powder, baking soda, and salt. Mix well to ensure even distribution.
3. In a separate bowl, whisk together the eggs (or flax seed mixture), milk (or almond milk), olive oil (or coconut oil), and honey (or maple syrup) until smooth.
4. Pour the wet mixture into the dry mixture and stir until just combined. Be careful not to overmix; a few lumps are fine.
5. Pour the batter into the prepared loaf pan, smoothing the top with a spatula.
6. Bake in the preheated oven for 20-25 minutes, or until the top is golden brown and a toothpick inserted into the center comes out clean.
7. Let the bread cool in the pan for 5-10 minutes before transferring to a wire rack to cool completely.

Variants and substitutions:

For a savory bread, add 1 teaspoon dried herbs (like rosemary or thyme) or spices (like garlic powder) to the dry ingredients. Use ground flax seed mixture for the eggs and almond milk to keep the recipe dairy-free. Stir in mashed banana or applesauce for a moist texture and natural sweetness.

Nutritional information (per serving): Calories: 150 kcal; Fiber: 4g; Net Carbs: 8g; Fat: 10g; Protein: 5g; Sugar: 2g; Cholesterol: 0g; Sodium: 120mg.

Quinoa and Black Bean Salad

Time: *10 min* ***Cook:*** *15 min* ***Serving****: 1*

Ingredients:

- Quinoa: ¼ cup (dry)
- Black beans: ½ cup (cooked or canned, rinsed and drained)
- Red bell pepper: ¼ cup, diced
- Cucumber: ¼ cup, diced
- Red onion: 1 tbsp, finely chopped
- Fresh cilantro: 2 tbsp, chopped (optional)
- Olive oil: 1 tbsp (or avocado oil)
- Lime juice: 1 tbsp (freshly squeezed)
- Cumin: ½ tsp
- Garlic powder: ¼ tsp
- Salt: to taste
- Black pepper: to taste
- Avocado: ¼, diced (optional)
- Corn: 2 tbsp (optional, canned or fresh)

Instructions:

1. Rinse quinoa under cold water to remove bitterness. In a small saucepan, bring 1/2 cup water to a boil. Add quinoa, reduce heat, cover, and simmer for 12 to 15 minutes until all water is absorbed. Remove from heat and fluff with a fork.
2. While quinoa cooks, prepare remaining ingredients. In a large bowl, combine black beans, diced red bell pepper, cucumber, red onion, and fresh cilantro (if using).
3. In a small bowl, whisk together olive oil, lime juice, cumin, garlic powder, salt, and black pepper.
4. Once quinoa is cooked and slightly cooled, add to the vegetable mixture. Pour dressing over salad and toss gently until well combined.
5. For extra flavor and texture, add diced avocado and corn (if using).
6. Serve immediately as a warm salad, or chill in the refrigerator for 15-20 minutes if you prefer it cold. Garnish with additional cilantro or lime wedges, if desired.

Variants and substitutions:

For a protein boost, add grilled chicken, shrimp, or tofu. Swap the quinoa for cauliflower rice for a low-carb alternative. Add cherry tomatoes, diced zucchini, or spinach for more nutrients.

Nutritional information (per serving): Calories: 320 kcal; Fiber: 12g; Net Carbs: 30g; Fat: 12g; Protein: 10g; Sugar: 3g; Cholesterol: 0g; Sodium: 180mg.

Mediterranean Chickpea Salad

Time: *10 min* ***Serving****: 1*

Ingredients:

- Chickpeas: ½ cup (canned, rinsed and drained)
- Cucumber: ¼ cup, diced
- Tomatoes: ¼ cup, halved
- Red onion: 1 tbsp, finely chopped
- Kalamata olives: 4-5, pitted and halved
- Feta cheese: 2 tbsp, crumbled (optional or use dairy-free feta)
- Fresh parsley: 1 tbsp, chopped
- Olive oil: 1 tbsp (or avocado oil)
- Lemon juice: 1 tbsp (freshly squeezed)
- Garlic powder: ¼ tsp
- Dried oregano: ¼ tsp
- Low-sodium salt: a pinch
- Pepper: to taste

Instructions:

1. In a large bowl, combine the chickpeas, diced cucumber, halved cherry tomatoes, finely chopped red onion, and Kalamata olives.
2. In a small bowl, whisk together the olive oil, lemon juice, garlic powder, dried oregano, salt, and pepper. Adjust seasoning to taste.
3. Pour the dressing over the chickpea mixture and toss gently to make sure everything is well coated.
4. Add crumbled feta and chopped parsley for extra flavor and freshness.
5. Serve immediately as a satisfying lunch, snack, or side dish. Enjoy at room temperature or chilled.

Variants and substitutions:

Add grilled chicken, turkey, or tofu for extra protein. Replace the feta with a dairy-free cheese or leave it out altogether for a vegan version. Feel free to add bell peppers, artichoke hearts, or spinach for more variety and nutrition.

Nutritional information (per serving): Calories: 280 kcal; Fiber: 8g; Net Carbs: 21g; Fat: 15g; Protein: 8g; Sugar: 5g; Cholesterol: 0g; Sodium: 300mg.

Mixed Greens with Grilled Chicken Salad

Time: *10 min* ***Cook:*** *15 min* ***Serving****: 1*

Ingredients:

- Mixed greens (spinach, arugula, or romaine): 2 cups
- Boneless, skinless chicken breast: 1 small (about 4 ounces)
- Olive oil: 1 tbsp (or avocado oil)
- Cherry tomatoes: ¼ cup, halved
- Cucumber: ¼ cup, sliced
- Red onion: 1 tbsp, thinly sliced
- Avocado: ¼, sliced
- Feta cheese: 1 tbsp, crumbled (optional)
- Balsamic vinegar: 1 tbsp
- Dijon mustard: 1 tsp
- Garlic powder: ¼ tsp
- Low-sodium salt: a pinch
- Pepper: to taste

Instructions:

1. Rub the chicken breast with 1 teaspoon of the olive oil, garlic powder, salt, and pepper.
2. Heat a grill or regular skillet over medium heat and cook the chicken breast for about 6-7 minutes on each side. Set aside and let rest for a few minutes before slicing.
3. In a large bowl, add the mixed greens, cherry tomatoes, cucumber, red onion, and avocado slices.
4. In a small bowl, whisk together the remaining olive oil, balsamic vinegar, Dijon mustard, salt, and pepper.
5. Arrange the sliced grilled chicken on top of the mixed greens. Drizzle the balsamic vinaigrette over the salad and garnish with crumbled feta cheese, if using.
6. Toss gently to combine and serve immediately.

Variants and substitutions:

Swap the chicken for grilled shrimp, salmon, or a plant-based option like tofu or tempeh for different dietary preferences. Omit the feta cheese or use a dairy-free alternative to make the salad vegan.

Nutritional information (per serving): Calories: 350 kcal; Fiber: 5g; Net Carbs: 7g; Fat: 22g; Protein: 28g; Sugar: 5g; Cholesterol: 85mg; Sodium: 350mg.

Tomato, Avocado and Cucumber Salad

Time: *10 min* ***Serving****: 1*

Ingredients:

- Cherry Tomatoes: ½ cup, halved (or diced Roma tomatoes)
- Cucumber: ½ cup, diced
- Avocado: ½, diced
- Red Onion: 2 tbsp, finely chopped
- Fresh Cilantro or Parsley: 1 tbsp, chopped (optional)
- Olive Oil: 1 tbsp (or avocado oil)
- Lime Juice: 1 tbsp (or lemon juice)
- Garlic Powder: ¼ tsp
- Low-sodium salt: a pinch
- Pepper: to taste

Instructions:

1. In a medium bowl, combine the halved cherry tomatoes, diced cucumber, and diced avocado. Add the diced red onion and chopped fresh herbs (cilantro or parsley), if using.
2. In a small bowl, whisk together the olive oil, lime juice, garlic powder, salt, and pepper. Adjust the seasoning to taste.
3. Pour the dressing over the salad mixture and gently toss everything together, being careful not to mash the avocado. Serve immediately.

Variants and substitutions:

For a heartier meal, you can add grilled chicken, shrimp, or a handful of cooked chickpeas or black beans. Try adding diced bell peppers or radishes for a crunchy touch. If you prefer, replace the cilantro or parsley with basil or dill for a different flavor profile.

Nutritional information (per serving): Calories: 220 kcal; Fiber: 8g; Net Carbs: 7g; Fat: 18g; Protein: 2g; Sugar: 4; Cholesterol: 0g; Sodium: 150mg.

Greek Sald with Lemon Vinaigrette

Time: *10 min* ***Serving****: 1*

Ingredients:

- Cucumber: ½ medium, cut into half moons
- Cherry tomatoes: ½ cup, halved (or diced Roma tomatoes)
- Red onion: 2 tbsp, thinly sliced
- Kalamata olives: ¼ cup, pitted and halved
- Feta cheese: ¼ cup, crumbled (optional for those who can consume dairy)
- Green bell pepper: ¼ cup, thinly sliced (optional)
- Romaine lettuce: 1 cup, chopped (optional for a heartier salad)
- Fresh oregano: 1 tsp, minced (or ¼ teaspoon dried oregano)

Lemon vinaigrette:

- Olive oil: 1 tbsp (or avocado oil)
- Lemon juice: 1 tbsp, freshly squeezed
- Dijon mustard: ½ tsp
- Garlic: 1 small clove, minced
- Low-sodium salt: a pinch
- Pepper: to taste

Instructions:

1. In a medium bowl, combine the cucumber, cherry tomatoes, red onion, Kalamata olives, and green bell pepper. Add the feta and fresh oregano.
2. In a small bowl, whisk together the olive oil, lemon juice, Dijon mustard, minced garlic, salt, and pepper. Adjust the dressing to taste.
3. Pour the lemon vinaigrette over the salad and toss gently until all the ingredients are coated. Serve immediately.

Variants and substitutions:

For a heartier meal, top the salad with grilled chicken, shrimp, or chickpeas for a veggie option. Swap the oregano for fresh basil, parsley, or dill for a different herbaceous flavor.

Nutritional information (per serving): Calories: 220 kcal; Fiber: 6g; Net Carbs: 9g; Fat: 35g; Protein: 4g; Sugar: 6g; Cholesterol: 0g; Sodium: 400mg.

30-DAYS MEAL PLAN

A 30-day meal plan is a comprehensive guide that structures daily meals to effectively manage blood sugar levels. A meal plan is essential to achieving and maintaining health, especially for people with conditions such as prediabetes, type 1 and type 2 diabetes.

The main benefits of a structured meal plan include:

- ➔ **Blood sugar management:** Helps control carbohydrate intake, which is essential for maintaining stable blood sugar levels.
- ➔ **Balanced nutrients:** A well-planned diet provides essential nutrients (protein, fiber, healthy fats) that support overall health while minimizing excess sugar and refined carbohydrates.
- ➔ **Portion control:** Structured plans prevent overeating, supporting weight management, a key factor in diabetes management.
- ➔ **Sustained energy:** By balancing macronutrients, people can avoid energy crashes and maintain consistent energy throughout the day.

The meal plan provided is an example. It should be tailored to your body type, gender, age, height, occupation and lifestyle.

For people with diabetes, carbohydrates should make up 45% to 65% of total daily calories. However, this can vary depending on individual needs and dietary goals. Assuming an average daily intake of about 1,000 calories, this translates to an intake of about 70 to 80 grams of carbohydrates per day. For an overweight person, for example, a low-calorie diet is preferable.

As for sugar intake, there is no unequivocal recommendation on how much to consume. Often, attention is paid instead to the type of carbohydrates consumed. It is generally recommended to limit the intake of added sugars and focus on carbohydrates from fruit, vegetables, whole grains and legumes.

The diet, therefore, should always be personalized by an expert, taking into account the eating habits of the individual and the family and their social life needs. It is therefore essential to always seek the advice of an expert.

This guide does not have the presumption or function of replacing the work of an expert (dietician or nutritionist) who must always be consulted to have an ad hoc nutritional plan.

1st day

Breakfast	Scrambled Eggs (p.18)
Lunch	Grilled Chicken And Vegetable Skewers (p.28)
Dessert	No-Bake Almond Butter Balls (p.65)
Dinner	Whole Wheat Pasta With Vegetables And Lean Protein (p.63)
Bread	Bread With Coconut Flour And Hemp Seed (p.81)
Beverage	Turmeric Milk (GOLDEN Milk) (p.70)

2nd day

Breakfast	High-Fiber Whole Grain Cereal (p.19)
Lunch	Lentil Soup With Spinach And Tomatoes (p.29)
Dessert	Baked Cinnamon Apples (p.66)
Dinner	Baked Tilapia With Lemon And Herbs (p.59)
Bread	Coconut Flour Bread (p.81)
Beverage	Sugar-Free Berry Smoothie (p.71)

3rd day

Breakfast	Oatmeal With Cinnamon And Berries (p.20)
Lunch	Baked Salmon With Asparagus (p.30)
Dessert	Sugar-Free Lemon Cheesecake (p.67)
Dinner	Spicy Lentil Soup (p.58)
Bread	Flax Seed Bread (p.82)
Beverage	Herbal Iced Tea With Lemon And Mint (p.72)

4th day

Breakfast	Spinach Smoothie (p.21)
Lunch	Broccoli And Chicken Stir-fry (p.31)
Dessert	Avocado Chocolate Mousse (p.68)
Dinner	Stuffed Peppers With Ground Turkey And Quinoa (p.57)
Bread	Whole Wheat Oatmeal Bread (p.83)
Beverage	Spicy Apple Cider Vinegar Drink (p.73)

5th day

Breakfast	Greek Yogurt Parfait (p.22)
Lunch	Spicy Grilled Shrimp And Vegetable Skewers (p.32)
Dessert	Raspberry Coconut Bars (p.69)
Dinner	Vegetable And Bean Soup (p.56)
Bread	Chia Seed And Almond Bread (p.84)
Beverage	Homemade Almond Milk (p.74)

6th day

Breakfast	Avocado Toast With Eggs (p. 23)
Lunch	Grilled Salmon With Cucumber Salad (p.33)
Dessert	No-Bake Almond Butter Balls (p.65)
Dinner	Herb-Roasted Chicken Thighs (p.54)
Bread	Almond Flour Bread (p.80)
Beverage	Turmeric Milk (GOLDEN Milk) (p.70)

7th day

Breakfast	Veggie Omelette (p.24)
Lunch	Zucchini Noodles With Tomato Sauce (p.34)
Dessert	Baked Cinnamon Apples (p.66)
Dinner	Grilled Vegetable Salad With Feta (p.52)
Bread	Coconut Flour Bread (p.81)
Beverage	Sugar-Free Berry Smoothie (p.71)

8th day

Breakfast	Almond Flour Pancakes (p. 25)
Lunch	Cauliflower Fried Rice (p.35)
Dessert	Sugar-Free Lemon Cheesecake (p.67)
Dinner	Chicken Fajitas With Grilled Peppers And Onions (p.51)
Bread	Flaxseed Bread (p.82)
Beverage	Herbal Iced Tea With Lemon And Mint (p.72)

9th day

Breakfast	Chia Seed Pudding (p.26)
Lunch	Baked Apple With Cinnamon And Nuts (p.36)
Dessert	Avocado Chocolate Mousse (p.68)
Dinner	Tofu And Broccoli Stir-Fry (p.48)
Bread	Whole Wheat Oatmeal Bread (p.83)
Beverage	Spicy Apple Cider Vinegar Drink (p.73)

10th day

Breakfast	Spinach And Feta Breakfast Wrap (p.27)
Lunch	Hearty Vegetable Soup (p.37)
Dessert	Raspberry Coconut Bars (p.69)
Dinner	Eggplant And Tomato Baked (p.49)
Bread	Chia Seed And Almond Bread (p.84)
Beverage	Homemade Almond Milk (p.74)

11th day

Breakfast	Scrambled Eggs (p.18)
Lunch	Stuffed Bell Peppers (p.38)
Dessert	No-Bake Almond Butter Balls (p.65)
Dinner	Vegetable And Bean Soup (p.56)
Bread	Almond Flour Bread (p.80)
Beverage	Turmeric Milk (GOLDEN Milk) (p.70)

12th day

Breakfast	High-Fiber Whole Grain Cereal (p.19)
Lunch	Turkey And Veggie Lettuce Wraps (p.39)
Dessert	Baked Cinnamon Apples (p.66)
Dinner	Spicy Lentil Soup (p.58)
Bread	Coconut Flour Bread (p.81)
Beverage	Herbal Iced Tea With Lemon And Mint (p.72)

13th day

Breakfast	Oatmeal With Cinnamon And Berries (p.20)
Lunch	Baked Cod With Lemon And Dill (p.41)
Dessert	Sugar-Free Lemon Cheesecake (p.67)
Dinner	Grilled Shrimp With Zucchini Noodles (p.46)
Bread	Flaxseed Bread (p.82)
Beverage	Spicy Apple Cider Vinegar Drink (p.73)

14th day

Breakfast	Spinach Smoothie (p.21)
Lunch	Roasted Vegetable Medley (p.42)
Dessert	Avocado Chocolate Mousse (p.68)
Dinner	Butternut Squash Soup (p.44)
Bread	Chia Seed And Almond Bread (p.84)
Beverage	Homemade Almond Milk (p.74)

15th day

Breakfast	Greek Yogurt Parfait (p.22)
Lunch	Turkey And Spinach Meatballs (p.43)
Dessert	Raspberry Coconut Bars (p.69)
Dinner	Hearty Vegetable Soup (p.37)
Bread	Coconut Flour Bread (p.81)
Beverage	Sugar-Free Berry Smoothie (p.71)

16th day

Breakfast	Avocado Toast With Eggs (p. 23)
Lunch	Tofu And Broccoli Stir-Fry (p.48)
Dessert	No-Bake Almond Butter Balls (p.65)
Dinner	Baked Apple With Cinnamon And Nuts (p.36)
Bread	Almond Flour Bread (p.80)
Beverage	Turmeric Milk (GOLDEN Milk) (p.70)

17th day

Breakfast	Veggie Omelette (p.24)
Lunch	Eggplant And Tomato Baked (p.49)
Dessert	Baked Cinnamon Apples (p.66)
Dinner	Zucchini Noodles With Tomato Sauce (p.34)
Bread	Coconut Flour Bread (p.81)
Beverage	Sugar-Free Berry Smoothie (p.71)

18th day

Breakfast	Almond Flour Pancakes (p. 25)
Lunch	Stir-Fried Tofu With Mixed Vegetables (p.50)
Dessert	Sugar-Free Lemon Cheesecake (p.67)
Dinner	Grilled Salmon With Cucumber Salad (p.33)
Bread	Flaxseed Bread (p.82)
Beverage	Herbal Iced Tea With Lemon And Mint (p.72)

19th day

Breakfast	Chia Seed Pudding (p.26)
Lunch	Chicken Fajitas With Grilled Peppers And Onions (p.51)
Dessert	Avocado Chocolate Mousse (p.68)
Dinner	Spicy Grilled Shrimp And Vegetable Skewers (p.32)
Bread	Whole Wheat Oatmeal Bread (p.83)
Beverage	Spicy Apple Cider Vinegar Drink (p.73)

20th day

Breakfast	Spinach And Feta Breakfast Wrap (p.27)
Lunch	Grilled Vegetable Salad With Feta (p.52)
Dessert	Raspberry Coconut Bars (p.69)
Dinner	Baked Salmon With Asparagus (p.30)
Bread	Chia Seed And Almond Bread (p.84)
Beverage	Homemade Almond Milk (p.74)

21ST day

Breakfast	Scrambled Eggs (p.18)
Lunch	Baked Lemon Garlic Chicken (p. 53)
Dessert	No-Bake Almond Butter Balls (p.65)
Dinner	Lentil Soup With Spinach And Tomatoes (p.29)
Bread	Almond Flour Bread (p.80)
Beverage	Turmeric Milk (GOLDEN Milk) (p.70)

22th day

Breakfast	High-Fiber Whole Grain Cereal (p.19)
Lunch	Herb-Roasted Chicken Thighs (p.54)
Dessert	Baked Cinnamon Apples (p.66)
Dinner	Whole Wheat Pasta With Vegetables And Lean Protein (p.63)
Bread	Coconut Flour Bread (p.81)
Beverage	Sugar-Free Berry Smoothie (p.71)

23rd day

Breakfast	Oatmeal With Cinnamon And Berries (p.20)
Lunch	Balsamic Glazed Salmon (p.55)
Dessert	Sugar-Free Lemon Cheesecake (p.67)
Dinner	Spicy Pumpkin Soup (p.64)
Bread	Flax Seed Bread (p.82)
Beverage	Herbal Iced Tea With Lemon And Mint (p.72)

24th day

Breakfast	Spinach Smoothie (p.21)
Lunch	Vegetable And Bean Soup (p.56)
Dessert	Avocado Chocolate Mousse (p.68)
Dinner	Chicken And Vegetable Stir-Fry (p.60)
Bread	Whole Wheat Oatmeal Bread (p.83)
Beverage	Spicy Apple Cider Vinegar Drink (p.73)

25th day

Breakfast	Greek Yogurt Parfait (p.22)
Lunch	Stuffed Peppers With Ground Turkey And Quinoa (p.57)
Dessert	Raspberry Coconut Bars (p.69)
Dinner	Tomato And Basil Soup (p.62)
Bread	Chia Seed And Almond Bread (p.84)
Beverage	Homemade Almond Milk (p.74)

26th day

Breakfast	Avocado Toast With Eggs (p. 23)Spicy Lentil Soup (p.58)
Lunch	Spicy Lentil Soup (p.58)
Dessert	No-Bake Almond Butter Balls (p.65)
Dinner	Baked Tilapia With Lemon And Herbs (p.59)
Bread	Almond Flour Bread (p.80)
Beverage	Turmeric Milk (GOLDEN Milk) (p.70)

27th day

Breakfast	Veggie Omelette (p.24)
Lunch	Balsamic Glazed Salmon (p.55)
Dessert	Baked Cinnamon Apples (p.66)
Dinner	Chickpea And Vegetable Curry (p.45)
Bread	Coconut Flour Bread (p.81)
Beverage	Sugar-Free Berry Smoothie (p.71)

28th day

Breakfast	Almond Flour Pancakes (p. 25)
Lunch	Chicken And Vegetable Stir-Fry (p.60)
Dessert	Sugar-Free Lemon Cheesecake (p.67)
Dinner	Cauliflower Fried Rice (p.35)
Bread	Flaxseed Bread (p.82)
Beverage	Herbal Iced Tea With Lemon And Mint (p.72)

29th day

Breakfast	Chia Seed Pudding (p.26)
Lunch	Chicken And Barley Soup (p.61)
Dessert	Avocado Chocolate Mousse (p.68)
Dinner	Grilled Salmon With Cucumber Salad (p.33)
Bread	Flaxseed Bread (p.82)
Beverage	Spicy Apple Cider Vinegar Drink (p.73)

30th day

Breakfast	Spinach And Feta Breakfast Wrap (p.27)
Lunch	Spicy Pumpkin Soup (p.64)
Dessert	Raspberry Coconut Bars (p.69)
Dinner	Grilled Chicken And Vegetable Skewers (p.28)
Bread	Whole Wheat Oatmeal Bread (p.83)
Beverage	Homemade Almond Milk (p.74)

CREATE YOUR OWN DIABETES-FRIENDLY RECIPE

By following these steps, you can use the knowledge you gain from the cookbook to create personalized, delicious, diabetes-friendly recipes. You can use your creativity and imagination to create recipes.

Step 1 - Review basic knowledge from the cookbook:

- Nutrition Principles: Revisit the chapters on low-sugar and low-carbs principles.
- Cooking Techniques: Remember basic cooking methods such as grilling, baking, steaming and sauteing.

Step 2 - Select ingredients that align with diabetic dietary guidelines:

- Protein: lean meats, fish, tofu, beans and legumes.
- Vegetables: Non-starchy vegetables such as leafy greens, broccoli, peppers and zucchini.
- Carbohydrates: Whole grains, quinoa, sweet potatoes and other complex carbohydrates.
- Fats: Healthy fats like avocados, nuts, seeds and olive oil.
- Spices and herbs: Experiment with herbs and spices to enhance flavor without adding sugar.

Step 3 - Decide on the type of meal you want to create:

- Breakfast: Consider options like vegetable omelets, whole-grain toast, or Greek yogurt with berries.
- Lunch: Think lean protein salads, whole grain sandwiches, or hearty vegetable soups.
- Dinner: Make grilled fish with roasted vegetables, stir-fried chicken with brown rice, or lentil stew.

Step 4 - Make sure your meal is well balanced:

- Half plate: non-starchy vegetables.
- A quarter of the plate: lean protein.
- One-quarter of the plate: whole grains or starchy vegetables.

Step 5 - Use the nutritional information in the recipe book as a reference or you can consult on the internet

- Portion Control: Measure portions to track your carb and calorie intake.
- Nutritional balance: Make sure the meal contains balanced macronutrients (protein, fat, carbohydrates) and adequate fiber.

Step 6 - Incorporates various flavors while keeping it diabetes-friendly:

- Natural sweeteners: Use cinnamon, vanilla, or a small amount of natural sweeteners like stevia.
- Herbs and spices: Add flavor without adding sugar or salt, for example by using garlic, ginger, turmeric or coriander.

Step 7 - Follow your plan and prepare the ingredients:

- Cooking method: Choose healthy cooking methods such as baking, grilling, steaming or sauteing.
- Consistency: Maintain consistency with how ingredients are prepared to ensure accurate nutritional content.

Step 8 - Taste your creation and make any necessary adjustments:

- Flavor adjustments: Add more spices or herbs if needed.
- Texture Adjustments: Adjust cooking times to achieve your desired texture.

Step 9 - Write your recipe:

- Ingredient list: Include all ingredients with their measured quantities.
- Step by step instructions: Clearly details the cooking process.
- Nutrition information: Calculate and include the nutritional breakdown per serving.

Step 10 - Share your new recipe with others:

- Family and friends: Enjoy your meal with your loved ones.
- Community: Consider sharing your recipe with the diabetes community for feedback and inspiration.

A Practical Example: Stir-Fried Chicken and Vegetables

Step 1: Review basic cookbook knowledge:

- Nutritional principles: guarantee balanced macronutrients and low sugar and carbohydrate content.
- Cooking techniques: Pan-frying is a quick and healthy cooking method.

Step 2: Select ingredients that align with diabetic dietary guidelines:

- Protein: chicken breast (lean protein)
- Vegetables: broccoli, peppers, carrots and sugar snap peas (non-starchy vegetables)
- Carbohydrates: brown rice (whole grains)
- Fats: olive oil (healthy fat)
- Spices and herbs: garlic, ginger, low-sodium soy sauce and fresh cilantro

Step 3: Decide on the type of meal you want to create:

- Dinner: Stir-fried chicken and vegetables with brown rice

Step 4: Make sure your meal is well balanced:

- Half plate: Mixed vegetables sautéed
- A quarter of the plate: sliced chicken breast
- A quarter of the plate: brown rice

Step 5: Use the nutritional information from the recipe book as a reference:

- Portion Control: Measure portions to track your carbs and calorie intake.
- Chicken breast: 4 oz
- Vegetables: 2 cups
- Brown rice: ½ cup cooked

Step 6: Incorporate various flavors while keeping it diabetes-friendly:

- Natural Sweeteners: Use a small amount of fresh ginger and garlic for natural sweetness and flavor.
- Herbs and spices: Add fresh cilantro at the end for a burst of freshness.

Step 7: Follow your plan and prepare the ingredients:

Ingredients:

- 1 pound chicken breast, cut into thin slices
- 2 cups broccoli florets
- 1 red bell pepper, sliced
- 1 carrot, julienned
- 1 cup sweet peas
- 1 tablespoon olive oil
- 2 cloves garlic, minced
- 1 tablespoon fresh ginger, chopped
- 2 tablespoons low-sodium soy sauce
- ¼ cup fresh cilantro, chopped
- ½ cup cooked brown rice

Cooking method: sauteed

- Heat the olive oil in a large skillet or wok over medium-high heat.
- Add the garlic and ginger and saute until fragrant.
- Add chicken slices, cook until no longer pink.
- Add broccoli, peppers, carrots and peas. Fry until the vegetables are tender and crunchy.
- Add the low-sodium soy sauce and mix well.
- Serve stir-fried over cooked brown rice.
- Garnish with fresh cilantro.

Step 8: Taste your creation:

- For more flavor, add a little more soy sauce or a pinch of pepper.
- Make sure the vegetables are cooked to the tenderness you prefer.

Step 9: Write your recipe:

List of ingredients:

- 1 pound chicken breast, cut into thin slices
- 2 cups broccoli florets
- 1 red bell pepper, sliced
- 1 carrot, julienned
- 1 cup sweet peas
- 1 tablespoon olive oil
- 2 cloves garlic, minced
- 1 tablespoon fresh ginger, chopped
- 2 tablespoons low-sodium soy sauce
- ¼ cup fresh cilantro, chopped
- ½ cup cooked brown rice

Step by step instructions:

- Heat the olive oil in a large skillet or wok over medium-high heat.
- Add the garlic and ginger and saute until fragrant.
- Add chicken slices, cook until no longer pink.
- Add broccoli, peppers, carrots and peas. Fry until the vegetables are tender and crunchy.
- Add the low-sodium soy sauce and mix well.
- Serve stir-fried over cooked brown rice.
- Garnish with fresh cilantro.

Nutritional information:

- Per portion (recipe serves 4 people):
- Calories: 320
- Protein: 28 g
- Carbohydrates: 30 g
- Fiber: 6 g
- Sugars: 5 g
- Fat: 10 gr

CONCLUSION

In this culinary adventure, we've curated a collection of recipes designed to tantalize your taste buds, nourish your body, and support your dietary needs. With particular attention to flavor, variety, and conscious eating, this cookbook offers a calibrated series of topics.

A delicious range of breakfast options, from hearty to light and refreshing. With a wide range of choices, every morning becomes a culinary delight.

A range of vibrant and satisfying lunch options, perfect for refueling at midday. Dig into the Mediterranean quinoa salad or

savor the Asian-inspired kale slaw. Whether you're at home or on the go, these lunches are a tasty way to fuel your day.

Let's not forget about the guilt-free craving for sweets with our selection of delicious desserts. And finally to end the day with a nutritious and satisfying dinner. Plus a chapter on homemade bread.

Savor the scent of freshly baked bread with our homemade bread recipes. Perfect for sandwiches, toast or to accompany your favorite soups.

Stay hydrated with a selection of refreshing drinks that quench thirst without added sugar.

Complement meals with our range of side dishes. From roasted garlic cauliflower to spicy roasted chickpeas, these side dishes add an extra layer of flavor and nutrition to your dish.

This guide is intended as more than a simple cooking recipe book; is a guide to embracing a balanced and tasty approach to cooking and eating. Whether you're treating diabetes, seeking a healthier lifestyle, or simply looking for delicious recipes that

everyone can enjoy, this cookbook is your companion on the path to culinary excellence and wellness.

We extend our heartfelt thanks to all who contributed, including the talented chefs, nutritionists, and cooking enthusiasts who shared their expertise to make this cookbook a reality. May your kitchen fill with the delicious aromas and flavors of these recipes as you embark on your culinary journey to better health.

Dear readers, allow me to make one last heartfelt appeal to you, one that resonates deeply with our shared journey:

In the context of our interactions, I believe deeply in the transformative power of your feedback. You must understand the deeper meaning of your insights, for they hold the key to many enriching possibilities. Every word you share holds the potential to shape the very fabric of our offerings.

Whether your experiences have been brilliant or tempered by challenges, rest assured: your sincere voices are the guiding stars that steer our ship to excellence. Your honesty is the cornerstone of our continued evolution, illuminating the path to perfection.

But the influence of your feedback doesn't end there. Your sincere testimonies create an unbreakable bridge of transparency, a bridge that invites new travelers to embark on a similar journey. Your narratives are not mere words; they are life rafts that help other explorers navigate the vast sea of choices, ensuring they arrive safely at their desired destinations.

However, the magic doesn't just stop at practicality. As you share your thoughts, a lovely community begins to take shape, where connections are made, ideas flow freely, and wisdom is exchanged like precious treasures. You, dear readers, are the architects of this thriving community, a testament to the boundless power of collective knowledge.

In your honest reviews, you wield the sword of accountability. You remind us every day of our constant commitment to the

highest standards of quality. Bring to life our promise to exceed expectations and the limits of our potential.

So, with the utmost gratitude and anticipation, I implore you to be the author of this incredible narrative. Let your voices rise and let your stories be the wind beneath the wings of change. Together we will continue to climb the peaks of excellence and sail the seas of shared experiences.

Thank you, my esteemed readers, for being the heart and soul of our journey.